Guitar
for Beginners

Guitar
for Beginners

TOM FLEMING

METRO BOOKS
New York

METRO BOOKS
New York

An Imprint of Sterling Publishing
1166 Avenue of the Americas
New York, NY 10036

Editorial and design by
Amber Books Ltd
74–77 White Lion Street
London N1 9PF
www.amberbooks.co.uk

Consultant: Mark Batley
Project Editor: Sarah Uttridge
Designer: Brian Rust
Picture Research: Terry Forshaw

ISBN: 978-1-4351-5663-0

For information about custom editions, special sales, and premium and corporate purchases,
please contact Sterling Special Sales at 800-805-5489 or specialsales@sterlingpublishing.com.

Manufactured in China

2 4 6 8 10 9 7 5 3

www.sterlingpublishing.com

Picture Credits

All images © Amber Books except for the following:

Alamy: 7C, 8 (Zuma), 27 (Anthony John Thompson), 47 (Mark Bourdillon), 57 (Brigette Supernova/Outer Focus), 84 (Pictorial Press), 100 (Pictorial Press), 121 (Alamy Celebrity)

Ernie Ball: 11BR

Behringer: 89TR

Boss: 6L, 88L, 89L&C

Dreamstime: 21B (Aodaodaod), 115 (Camrocker), 122L (Reinhold68), 122R (Amlan Mathur)

Dunlop: 89B

Eno Music: 11TL, 20B

Epiphone: 16

Fender: 10R, 13BR, 17, 20T, 26, 96

Fotolia: 10BL (Khafioz Ruslan), 11CL (Africa Studio), 11BL (Bruno135), 11CR (Roman Gorielov). 12R (African Studio), 13TR (VolkOFF-ZS-BP), 15L (Elnur),
15TR (Your-lucky-stars), 15BR (Tiler84), 21T (Alexander Maximov), 21C (Tuulijumala), 25L (Phot65), 25R (Aleksey Kinyapin), 69T (Grandaded), 69B (Gilly Smith),
87T (Branislav Zivkovic), 87B (Lucky Dragon USA), 106 (Alenavlad), 123T (Gna60), 123B (Pavel Losevsky), 124 (Jaimie Duplass), 125T (Petair), 125B (Jipen)

Getty Images: 6R (Ebet Roberts), 7TR (David Redfern), 28 (Michael Ochs Archive), 48 (Peter Still), 58 (Richard E. Aaron), 70 (Gary Wolstenholme), 79 (Mark Venema),
97 (David Redfern), 110 (Mike Cameron), 126 (Michael Ochs Archive)

Gibson: 6C, 10TL, 14, 78, 120

Korg: 13L

Marshall: 7BR

C. F. Martin Archives: 7L, 46, 56

National Resonator: 67

Planet Waves: 11TR, 42

Rickenbacker: 12L

Voodoo Lab: 88R

CONTENTS

Introduction

Chapter 1: Guitar Basics   8

Chapter 2: Changing Chords   28

Chapter 3: Exploring Rhythms   48

Chapter 4: Getting Bluesy   58

Chapter 5: Barre Chords   70

Chapter 6: Lead Guitar and Rock 'n' Roll   84

Chapter 7: Fingerstyle Guitar   100

Chapter 8: Rock Guitar   110

Chapter 9: Chord Reference   126

Glossary   142
Index   143

INTRODUCTION

This book is designed to help you take the first steps on your journey as a guitarist. Whether you love rock, blues, jazz, metal or folk – or any other musical style – the basics of guitar playing are essentially the same. As a beginner there are many issues to consider and concepts to master.

One of the first things to consider is what kind of guitar you should buy. Acoustic or electric? Do you need an amp? What about other accessories such as a tuner, guitar stand, strap, cable and spare strings? This book aims to guide you through all of these questions and more.

Having invested in your first guitar and anything else you may need, it's time to start playing. The guitar can feel like an alien object to a beginner; certain skills have to be practised over and over again before the instrument begins to feel familiar. It's important to keep practising, but also to keep introducing new material, with enough musical variety that you stay interested. This book does just that.

This book is divided into chapters covering all the important skills and knowledge that any guitar player needs, in a range of styles from simple strumming to the basics of fingerpicking and rock 'n' roll rhythm playing.

POSTURE AND TECHNIQUE

We've tried to go easy on the music theory, but some areas of playing, both within the scope of this book and beyond, will benefit greatly from a little basic knowledge. Similarly, most guitar players are fairly relaxed about things like posture and precise left-hand technique, but again it is important to avoid certain

Les Paul
The Gibson Les Paul is one of the archetypal electric guitar designs. You may not be able to afford a real one, but many guitars are essentially based on this design.

Jack White
Jack White (formerly of The White Stripes and now a solo artist) has always put his raw, gutsy guitar playing right in the foreground on his minimally produced records.

Effects Pedals
These useful boxes are usually not expensive and provide a great way to expand the sounds at your disposal and access them easily.

pitfalls if you want to get years of musical satisfaction out of your chosen instrument and to avoid some basic errors that could lead to pain and injury if left unchecked.

PRACTICE SESSIONS

If you want to progress on the guitar, as with any advanced skill, the key word is practice. A little and often is better than longer, infrequent practice sessions: half an hour every day will give better results than a whole day once a week, particularly in the early stages. As a beginner, you will find your left-hand fingertips will easily become sore, and this can be painful. If you practise a little every day, your fingertips will develop calluses (pads of harder, thicker skin) and you will soon forget that playing was once painful. Until this happens, however, don't try to ignore the pain for too long: put the guitar down and return to it later, or work on some other skill or area of knowledge.

King Of The Blues
B.B. King's lyrical blues guitar style provided a template for generations of blues players and bands, including Eric Clapton.

Martin
CF Martin & Co invented the instrument we have come to call the steel-strung acoustic guitar, and all other acoustic guitar designs are based on the original design.

We've also added some information on inspirational guitarists – but rather than the 'usual suspects' (the loud, fast, muscular players who might spring to mind at first), we've decided to focus on some musicians who might provide more genuinely useful inspiration to a beginner.

Finally, the Chords Reference Section provides a handy reference point that should help you get through more songs of the kind featured in this book.

The Quiet One
George Harrison generally got less attention than the other Beatles, but by quietly getting on with playing the guitar he was essential to the band's evolving sound.

The Quintessential Rock Amp
Many smaller and quieter amps aim to emulate the sound of the Marshall Stack.

CHAPTER 1:

GUITAR BASICS

This chapter begins at the very beginning: choosing a guitar and other items, tuning, posture and the basics of left-hand and right-hand technique.

LEFT: Alex Turner of Arctic Monkeys

WHAT YOU NEED

To get started with the guitar, you will need a few other items. All of these can be easily found at almost any music store. Not everything here is immediately essential: you can get started with just a guitar, pick and tuner.

ACOUSTIC OR ELECTRIC GUITAR
(P. 12–13)

AMP.*
(P. 14–15)

CABLE.*
(P. 14–15)

* ONLY NEEDED WITH AN ELECTRIC GUITAR

STRING WINDER/ TRIMMER
(P. 42–43)

TUNER
(P. 12–13, 20–21)

STRAP
(P. 12–13)

PICKS/ PLECTRUMS
(P. 12–13)

SPARE STRINGS
(P. 42–43)

METRONOME
(P. 24–25)

CHOOSING A GUITAR AND ACCESSORIES

If you have not already bought a guitar, there are some things to think about before buying. Firstly: acoustic or electric? An acoustic guitar is in many ways the simplest choice, as it is a self-contained instrument requiring fewer accessories; the electric guitar requires an amp, and a cable to connect the two to make a fuller sound.

YOUR CHOICE OF GUITAR

On the other hand, the electric guitar is actually easier to play for most beginners, as the strings are slightly thinner and lower-tension, requiring less force to press them down.

Finally, your choice of guitar will probably be determined by the styles of music you ultimately wish to play. Either acoustic or electric guitar will be equally suitable for covering the material in this book and some way beyond, but if you intend to go further with electric guitar playing, and ultimately into sounds and techniques that simply do not translate on to the acoustic guitar, you may wish to start on electric from the outset. Equally, if you gravitate more towards acoustic styles, you may wish to get used to an acoustic guitar from the beginning.

FINGERTIPS

If you have tried an acoustic guitar and found that your fingers hurt, it could be worth considering an electric. However, practising a little each day will soon improve your finger strength and result in harder fingertips; once you have developed the strength for acoustic guitar, the electric guitar will seem relatively easy.

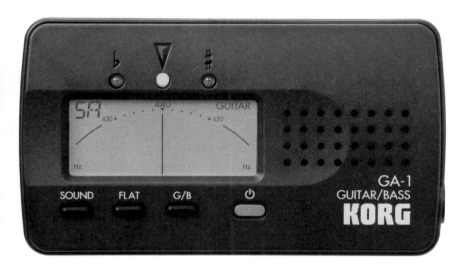

ACCESSORIES

TUNER

No matter how good your technique, an out-of-tune guitar will never sound good. Tuning is easier than ever as there are many inexpensive and effective tuners to choose from. Most of these will do the job for almost all guitars. If you have an acoustic guitar, choose a tuner with a built-in microphone. If you have an electric guitar, you will probably want a tuner with a direct input; this makes it easier to tune discreetly. For many players, the simplest solution for either type of instrument is a clip tuner; this attaches to the guitar (usually at the headstock) and picks up the vibrations of the guitar from the body.

TUNER APPS

You may not need a dedicated hardware tuner: if you have a smartphone, you can choose from a range of free or inexpensive tuner apps.

PICKS

Many guitar players use a pick (also known as a plectrum) most of the time. Some styles are based on fingerpicking (where the thumb and fingers of the right hand are used separately), but most pop and rock playing uses the pick, and you will need one straight away to get started with the strumming-based styles in this book.

Picks come in many thicknesses; medium gauge (around 0.7mm) is usually best for general use.

STRAP

You will probably sit down to practise, but it is often a good idea to use a strap to prevent the guitar from slipping – particularly with the electric guitar. Generally the strap should be adjusted so that it doesn't go slack when moving from standing to sitting, and the guitar remains in roughly the same area of the body. This will ensure that you do not try to wear the guitar either too high or too low when standing.

CHOOSING AN AMP

If you are using an acoustic guitar, you will not need an amp at this stage. If you have an electric guitar however, you will need some form of amplifier: the electric guitar makes very little sound of its own. Guitar amps come in many shapes and sizes, so which one should you buy?

Larger amps are designed to produce enough volume to compete with a drum kit and fill a large, noisy venue. These tend to be heavy and big, and you are unlikely to need all that volume as a beginner. The best amp for a beginner is a 'practice amp'. Most of the major amp manufacturers have a range of practice amps designed to look and sound like smaller versions of their gigging amps. Practice amps are smaller and lighter, and typically rated at 20W or less. They usually have plenty of volume for practising on your own or with another musician or singer.

PRACTICE AMPS

Like larger amps, many practice amps have two separate 'channels'. This means that there are two sets of controls, so you can set up separate sounds and change between them (usually using a footswitch) during a song. This is useful if you want to use a clean sound for most of the song, but want to add distortion (a guitar effect to create a fuzzy sound) for a solo section. Although you may not use distortion to begin with, it's worth looking at a two-channel amp from the outset.

WHAT IS A WATT?

An amplifier's power is measured in watts (W) – just like heaters and light bulbs! Normally, amps designed for use on big stages are rated at 100W or more, and practice amps as little as 1W. These figures don't always tell the whole story, however – there are some very loud amps available rated at 20W or less.

OTHER ACCESSORIES

CABLE

To connect your guitar to an amp, you will need a cable known as a jack cable. This is terminated at each end with a quarter-inch (6.35mm) mono jack plug. This is universally known simply as a guitar cable, and should be available from any music store. The very cheapest ones tend to be flimsy and offer poor sound quality, so it's worth spending a little more to get a stouter cable that will offer better sound quality and longer life. Make sure you get a cable that is long enough so that you can put the amp where you want it.

CASE/GIG BAG

If you plan to travel any distance at all with your guitar, a case is essential. A hard case offers the greatest protection, but will be more expensive and take up more space. Very thin soft cases offer little protection from anything other than rain; the best compromise is a thicker, padded soft case with shoulder straps, called a *gig bag*.

STAND

Protect your investment: a guitar left leaning against a wall or chair can very easily be knocked over and damaged. Even a cheap, basic stand will hold it much more securely.

THE ACOUSTIC GUITAR

The acoustic guitar is associated with many acoustic music styles that are generally derived from folk music. It is therefore very popular with self-accompanying singer-songwriters, and also commonly found in country and bluegrass music.

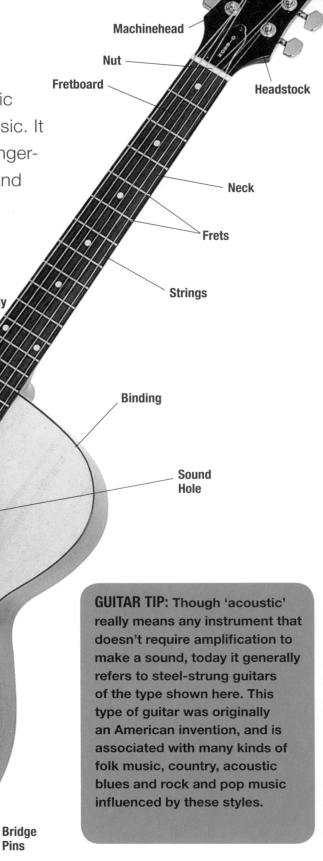

Tuning Peg

Machinehead

Nut

Fretboard

Headstock

Neck

Frets

Strings

Body

Saddle

Binding

Bridge

Sound Hole

Bridge Pins

GUITAR TIP: Though 'acoustic' really means any instrument that doesn't require amplification to make a sound, today it generally refers to steel-strung guitars of the type shown here. This type of guitar was originally an American invention, and is associated with many kinds of folk music, country, acoustic blues and rock and pop music influenced by these styles.

THE ELECTRIC GUITAR

The electric guitar is arguably the central instrument in almost all rock and pop music. Had it not been invented, the history of music would sound very different: imagine what The Beatles, The Rolling Stones, Led Zeppelin or Guns N' Roses would sound (and look) like without electric guitars...

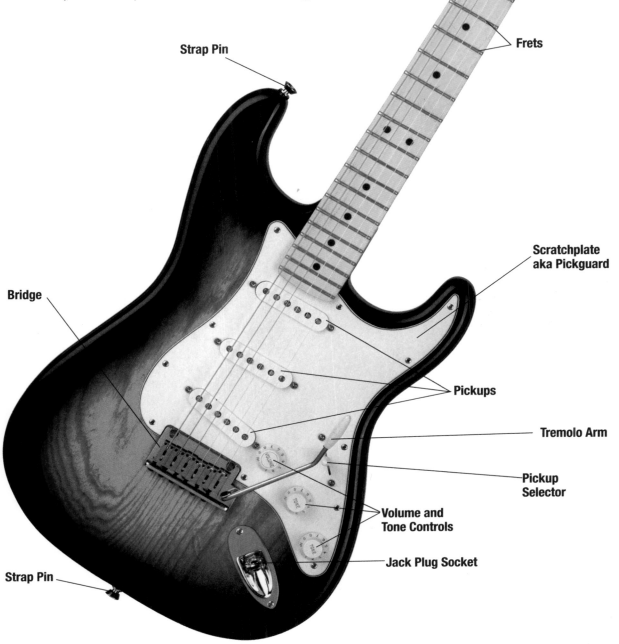

Tuning Peg

Machinehead

Nut

Headstock

Neck

Fretboard

Frets

Strap Pin

Bridge

Scratchplate
aka Pickguard

Pickups

Tremolo Arm

Pickup
Selector

Volume and
Tone Controls

Jack Plug Socket

Strap Pin

POSTURE

In the rock and pop world, posture (the way that you position your body) varies considerably between players; classical players and teachers tend to be much stricter. As a general rule, try to be as relaxed as possible: anything that feels uncomfortable is probably not a good idea.

RELAX

Try to be as relaxed as possible when playing the guitar. When sitting, place the guitar so that the curve in the side of the instrument's body sits naturally on your right leg. You may wish to use a strap even when sitting, particularly if you have an electric guitar. When standing, the strap is essential. It should be adjusted so that the guitar is neither very much higher nor very much lower in relation to the body than when sitting. Though many rock players wear the guitar much lower than this when standing, this is in fact potentially very bad for various parts of your body, particularly if your left wrist is forced into an unnatural shape.

CORRECT

INCORRECT

THE RIGHT HAND

The right hand holds the pick, which is used to strum or pick the strings. Strumming means playing more than one string at a time, often all six, generally with a large, relaxed motion of the whole forearm. Picking means playing one string at a time – usually using much smaller, more precise movements of the hand only.

HOLDING THE PICK

The pick is gripped between the thumb and index finger of the right hand. The thumb should be at approximately a right angle to the first joint of the index finger, with the pick in between. Generally only a few millimetres of the pick should protrude. Hold the pick just tightly enough to keep it in place when playing.

THE LEFT HAND

The fingers of the left hand press the strings down on to the fretboard, usually using the tip of the finger. When one string is pressed in a given place while the right hand picks the same string, a single note is produced. When the right hand strums across several strings, more than one note is produced. This is called a chord. Chords are made up of several fretted notes and/or several open strings.

The left-hand thumb should always make contact with the back of the neck. Rock and pop players aren't as strict about the thumb's exact position as classical players, but in general the thumb should be in contact with the neck's thickest point. Rock players often allow the thumb

GUITAR TIP: Throughout this book, we will use the terms 'left' and 'right' as they apply to a right-handed player. If you are left–handed, you will need a left-handed guitar. In that case, simply reverse all occurrences of 'left' and 'right'.

to wrap around the neck to some extent. This is fine as long as it doesn't accidentally stop strings from sounding (sometimes, you may use it to do this deliberately, and even on occasion to form part of a chord).

The fingers of the left hand should be allowed to hover in readiness above the fretboard when not actually playing notes or chords – avoid letting them stray to the side or underneath.

CORRECT

INCORRECT

TUNING

Every time you pick up the guitar to play, it is important to make sure that the strings are tuned properly. Some guitars lose their tuning more quickly than others, and as you gain experience you will develop the ability to check if your guitar is in tune by playing a chord or even just the open strings.

E
A
D
G
B
E

Out of Tune
You should check the tuning of your guitar after carrying it in a case because one or more of the machineheads can easily be turned accidentally, putting the guitar out of tune.

TUNING

To begin with you should tune each string using a tuner every time you play. The results of this will reward the effort: however good your playing, the guitar will only sound good if it is in tune.

Most modern tuners automatically display the nearest 'target' note to the pitch being sounded. Assuming that the strings haven't drifted very far since the last time the guitar was played, simply play each string in turn and check whether the display reads 'flat' (too low), 'sharp' (too high) or in tune (dead centre). If necessary, keep playing the string while adjusting its tension using the machinehead: make the string tighter to raise the pitch, and looser to lower it. When you have reached the correct pitch (dead centre), move on to the next string.

In case the strings *have* gone very far out of tune (as can happen when transporting an instrument, for example), or after changing strings (see p. 42-43), you will need to know the names of the open strings so that you don't accidentally tune the strings to the wrong pitches. From the lowest pitch (thickest string) to the highest, these are:

GUITAR TIP: Standard tuning is just one possibility, and other tunings can be a whole lot of fun. But just stick to the standard tuning to begin with.

Clip Tuner
This clip tuner captures vibrations from the guitar's headstock.

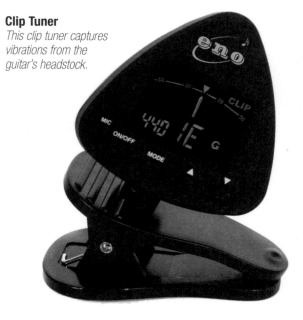

Low					High
E	A	D	G	B	e

PLUGGING IN

If you have an electric guitar, you will need to connect it to your amp and power up before you can play. All amps have slightly different sets of controls, so it is important to read the manual that came with yours for specific information on that model. In general, however, almost all amps have a master volume control. This is usually found to the right of the other controls, and represents the last part of the circuit. If the master volume is set to zero there will be no sound, whatever the settings of the other controls. So it is a good idea to set the master volume to zero before powering up, and then raise it slowly so you can hear what effect the other controls are having on the sound, and until you achieve the volume you want.

GUITAR TIP: Many amps can produce volumes that could damage your hearing. There is no need to use this much volume on your own; you may have to when playing with a full band including drums, in which case earplugs are essential.

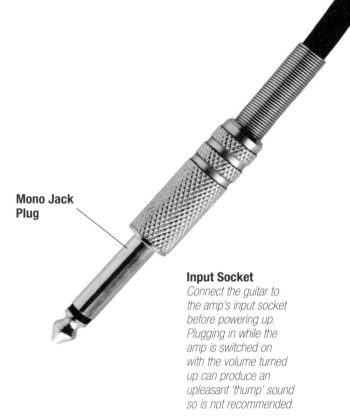

Mono Jack Plug

Input Socket
Connect the guitar to the amp's input socket before powering up. Plugging in while the amp is switched on with the volume turned up can produce an upleasant 'thump' sound so is not recommended.

1   2
INPUTS   VOLUME   TREBLE   BASS   DRIVE   VOLUME   CH SELECT   TREBLE   MID   MID CONTOUR   BASS   REVERB   FOOT SWITCH   PRE OUT   PWR IN

AMP CONTROLS

Gain: Turning up the gain increases the volume, but also begins to introduce distortion (sometimes known as overdrive). Distortion is used creatively in many guitar styles.

Vibrato: A wavering sound produced by shivering a fretted note up and down rapidly.

Reverb: The sound that remains or lingers after the original sound has stopped.

Bass/Middle/Treble: Can be used to make the sound brighter or warmer.

YOUR FIRST CHORD

A chord is a group of notes that sound good together. On the guitar, these usually have names that we associate with shapes on the fretboard.

CHORD BOXES

Chord boxes provide the simplest way to show how to play a chord. The box is really a grid, with six vertical lines representing the strings, and a number of horizontal lines representing frets. A thick horizontal line at the top represents the nut.

Don't play this string

Open strings

A

A
CHORD

X O   O

—— **Nut**

—— **1st fret**

❶❷❸ —— **Finger positions**

—— **2nd fret**

A number of dots are used to show where to place the fingers. For beginners, these are usually numbered, so you know exactly which fingers to use.

All we need to show how to play a basic chord is a box with these finger dots, and often just a few other symbols.

If there is no fingering dot on a string, it is either because the open string is part of the chord (shown with an 'O') or because the string should not be played in this chord (shown with an 'X').

The name of the chord is shown above the box.

Finger Numbers
Pay attention to the finger numbers shown for all of the chords in this book.

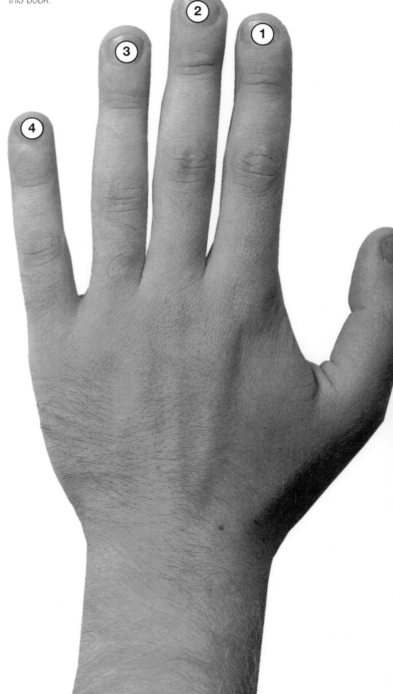

THE Em CHORD

Em CHORD

Em

This is one of the easiest chords to play on the guitar. The symbol 'Em' is short for *E minor*. Simple guitar chords are either major or minor (a letter on its own, such as A, C or G, indicates a major chord).

This chord uses two left-hand fingers: the second and third. The first and fourth fingers should not touch the strings, but they should hover above the fretboard in readiness for changing to other chords.

EM CHORD STRUMMING

Almost all music has a time signature: this is the number of beats that you would keep counting if you were counting along to the music. In most pop and rock music, this number is four, so we keep counting '1 2 3 4, 1 2 3 4, 1 2 3 4…'. Each group of four beats is known as a bar. In written music, bars are separated using vertical lines called barlines. The symbol 4/4 at the beginning shows that there are four beats per bar.

EXERCISE 1

Keep counting '1 2 3 4' and strum downwards across all six strings while playing the Em chord.

1. **Em**

| 4/4 | ↓ 1 | ↓ 2 | ↓ 3 | ↓ 4 | ↓ 1 | ↓ 2 | ↓ 3 | ↓ 4 | ↓ 1 | ↓ 2 | ↓ 3 | ↓ 4 | ↓ 1 | ↓ 2 | ↓ 3 | ↓ 4 |

STRUMMING EXERCISES

Strummed guitar parts involve a degree of coordination: the left hand must change chord shape every so often, while the right hand provides the rhythmic interest. To start with, we'll keep the left hand holding just one chord shape while the right hand plays some simple rhythms.

The exercises on these two pages all use just the Em chord.

While the time signature does not generally change within a song, this does not mean that you have to strum on every beat. In this book, we will progress gradually from very simple strumming ideas to more complex ones.

The time signatures here are either **4/4** (four beats per bar) or **3/4** (three beats per bar). Keep counting to either 4 or 3 as applicable, but strum only where shown. Where there is no strum on a beat, the chord should be allowed to sound: so chords may sound for one, two, three or four beats. This creates some simple rhythms.

REPEATS

Special barlines are used to show that a section of music should be repeated. These look like double barlines with two dots on one side or other, meaning 'start of repeated section' and 'end of repeated section'.

‖:   start repeat

:‖   end repeat

‖:   (repeat this material)   :‖

EXERCISES

1. Em

1. Em

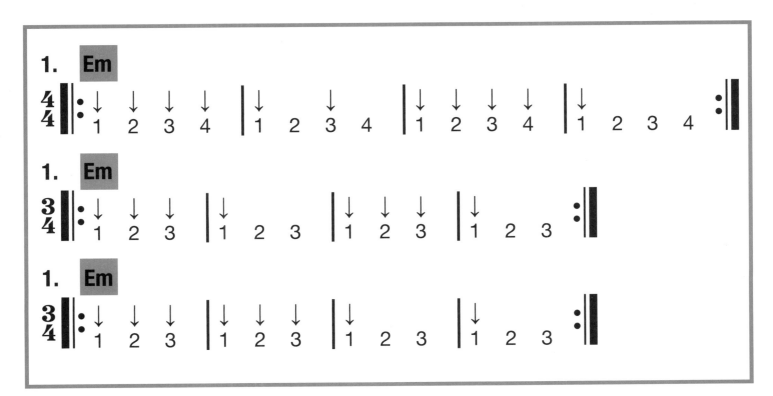

USING A METRONOME

The metronome is a convenient practice tool that makes a regular 'click' sound. Several different kinds are available, including old-fashioned mechanical types, modern digital models, and smartphone apps. The important thing is that the pulse timing is precise, and adjustable. Usually, this speed (known in music as 'tempo') is set in beats per minute (bpm). If you have a metronome or app, try playing these exercises at a tempo setting of around 80 bpm. Try to make sure each strum happens at exactly the same time as each click.

Pendulum

Mechanical Metronome
These tend to be more expensive than digital ones, but some people find them more satisfying to use.

Weight

Winder

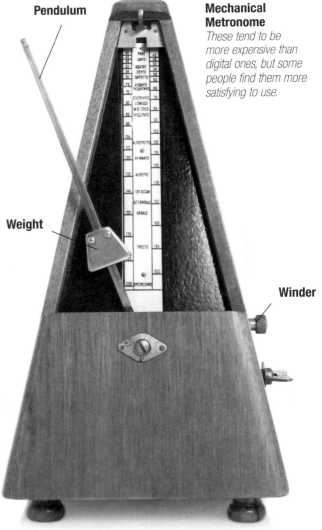

Digital Metronome
These tend to be cheaper and more flexible than mechanical ones; some even have a tuner built in.

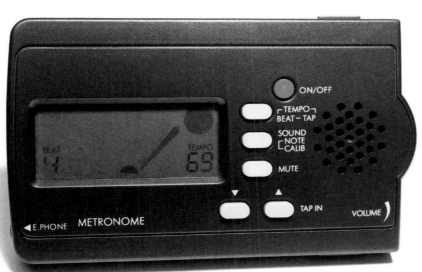

JAKE BUGG
1994–

RECOMMENDED LISTENING:

Jake Bugg (album)

Shangri-La (album)

Jake Bugg represents the latest generation of British guitar-based singer-songwriters, though his influences are broader than this might suggest. These would seem to include Donovan, The Beatles and Paul Simon, but the sound of British skiffle music also looms large. Bugg's records are often deliberately lo-fi, with guitar and vocals in particular sounding as though they were recorded in the early 1960s.

Bugg is equally at home on acoustic and electric guitar. His fingerpicking acoustic guitar style is firmly in the territory staked out in the 1960s by Paul Simon and British folk players such as Bert Jansch. On electric guitar, his style is often rockier – sometimes bluesy, and with more than a touch of the loud, brash sound of British punk.

Bugg first achieved public recognition after he was chosen to appear at the 2011 Glastonbury Festival, which led to a recording contract with Mercury Records. Two albums followed relatively quickly,

featuring collaborations with legendary producer Rick Rubin and Chad Smith of Red Hot Chili Peppers, with live and televised appearances on both sides of the Atlantic soon establishing Jake Bugg as a major artistic force for the second decade of the century.

During 2013 Jake Bugg was nominated for a raft of major awards, winning the coveted Q Awards' *Best New Act*.

Fender Telecaster
One of Jake Bugg's favoured electric guitars, the Telecaster provides an earthy twang perfectly suited to many of his songs.

JAKE BUGG FAVOURS SIMPLE, CLASSIC EQUIPMENT:

ACOUSTIC GUITARS BY MARTIN AND YAMAHA, AND ELECTRICS FROM FENDER, GIBSON AND GRETSCH.

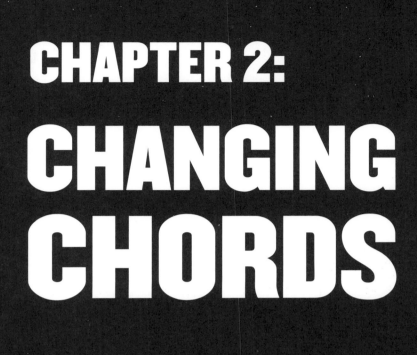

CHAPTER 2:

CHANGING CHORDS

Here we look at an essential skill for any player: however many chords you know, it is important to be able to change between them smoothly and in time.

LEFT: Buddy Holly and The Crickets

THE D CHORD

Our next chord is called D, or D major. This shape uses fingers 1, 2 and 3. The key of D is popular in folk music as it tends to suit the range of both male and female voices and because the D chord can be dressed up in various ways. To try this, lift the second finger so that the high E string is open, and then add it back in on the next beat.

D
CHORD

The D string in this chord is open ('O'). The two lowest strings (E and A) should not be played with the D chord ('X'). This can be achieved in two ways: firstly by avoiding them with the right hand, and only strumming the four strings that are used in the chord. Secondly, the thumb may wrap around the neck to touch the bottom strings to mute them. If you do this, be careful not to apply too much pressure: this would produce fretted notes, which are also unwanted here.

GUITAR TIP: Most songs use three or more chords. One of these, known as the tonic chord, defines the key of the song, so we say that the song is 'in the key of D' (for example). Usually, the tonic chord will appear more often than any other chord, and generally sounds like 'home' – as though the music comes to rest when this chord is reached.

CHANGING CHORDS

The greatest challenge for the beginner guitarist is to learn to change chords without holding up the flow of the music. To begin with, practise changing from Em to D in no particular rhythm. Strum the Em chord, allow it to ring, and then change as quickly as possible to the D chord. Pay attention to exactly what each finger needs to do to make the change, and try to make the movement as economical as possible.

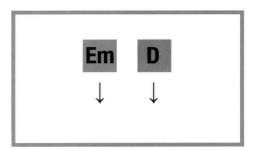

CHANGING IN TIME

Next, try to time the change so that you will be ready to play the chord at a precise point. Don't worry about strumming on every beat of the bar at this stage – one strum per bar (four beats) is enough. If you have a metronome, set it to around 80 bpm and count '1, 2, 3, 4' for each chord. As the chord sounds, try to prepare yourself for the chord change.

If you find this too challenging at first, try a slower tempo such as 60 bpm, or allow each chord to sound for two whole bars (8 beats) at first. (If you don't have a metronome, you can use the second hand of a watch or clock as a metronome fixed to 60 bpm.)

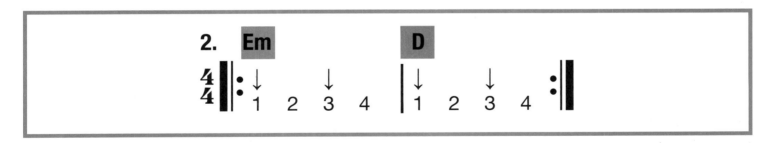

Once you have mastered this, move on to playing two strums per bar (beats 1 and 3).

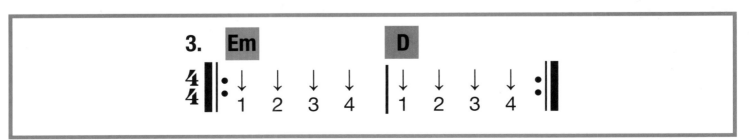

Next, move on to playing on every beat in the bar. Don't worry at this stage if the fourth beat gets cut off as you start to change. This will get smoother as you progress, but will never disappear entirely; there will always be small squeaks and scuffs – that's the sound of a real human being playing an instrument.

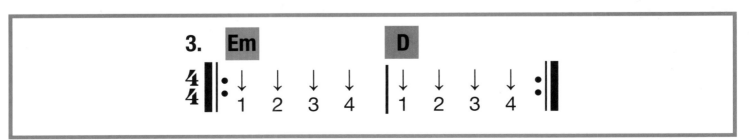

TWO NEW CHORDS: E AND A

Thousands of songs can be played using just three chords. If we combine two new chords with the D chord, we can play three chord songs in the key of A. The two new chords we need are E and A.

THE E CHORD

The E chord is like the Em chord with one different note: the first finger is added at the first fret of the G string. This one note changes the chord from major to minor. Try changing between them and listen to the quality of each chord. Major chords are sometimes described as sounding happy, whereas minor chords are said to sound sad. As with the Em chord, all six strings may be played.

THE A CHORD

The A chord is also similar to the Em chord: the second and third fingers retain the same formation, but on the next pair of strings (the D and G strings). The first finger frets the D string, second fret. The A and high E strings are open; the low E string should not be played.

E CHORD

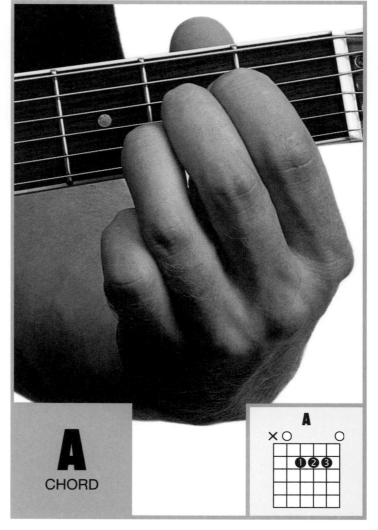

A CHORD

CHANGING CHORDS

The chords A, D and E belong together in the key of A, and in three-chord songs you might need them in any combination. Practise changing between all combinations of these chords:

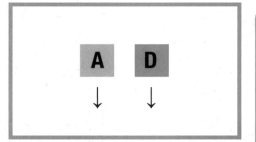

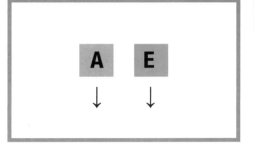

GUITAR TIP: Always aim for minimum finger movement when changing chords. For example, when changing from D to E or vice versa, the first finger doesn't need to be lifted from the fretboard, but may instead slide along the G string.

Remember to take advantage of the similarities between the A and E shapes: keep the second and third fingers 'locked' together as they move.

EXERCISES

These exercises are written with four strums per bar, but you may want to start by strumming once per bar, and then twice (see p. 31).

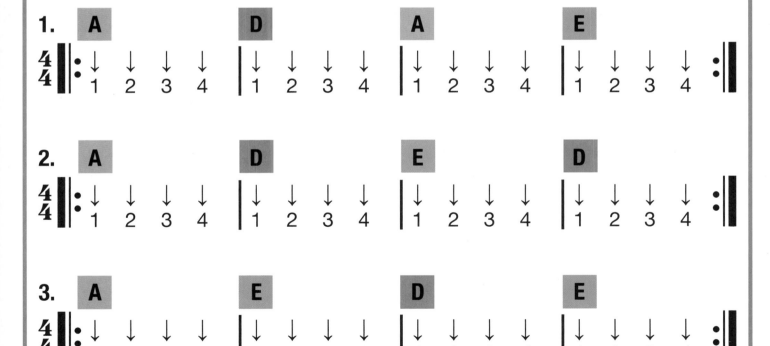

PLAY A SONG

Swing Low, Sweet Chariot

This traditional spiritual song has been covered by numerous artists including Elvis Presley, Johnny Cash and Eric Clapton. It's easy to play using just three chords, and is arranged here in the key of A (chords A, D and E).

CHORDS

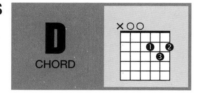

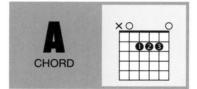

CHORD SEQUENCE

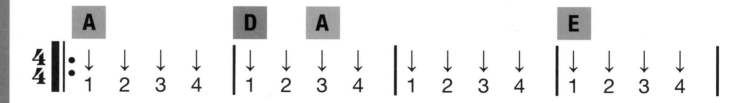

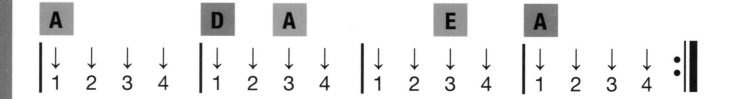

CHORUS

Swing low, sweet chariot

E
Coming for to carry me home,

Swing low, sweet chariot,

E   A
Coming for to carry me home.

VERSE 1

A   D   A
I looked over Jordan, and what did I see

E
Coming for to carry me home?

A   D   A
A band of angels coming after me,

E   A
Coming for to carry me home.

Repeat Chorus

VERSE 2

A   D   A
Sometimes I'm up, and sometimes I'm down,

E
(Coming for to carry me home)

A   D   A
But still my soul feels heavenly bound.

E   A
(Coming for to carry me home)

Repeat Chorus

VERSE 3

A   D   A
The brightest day that I can say,

E
(Coming for to carry me home)

A   D   A
When Jesus washed my sins away.

E   A
(Coming for to carry me home)

Repeat Chorus

VERSE 4

A   D   A
If I get there before you do,

E
(Coming for to carry me home)

A   D   A
I'll cut a hole and pull you through.

E   A
(Coming for to carry me home)

Repeat Chorus

VERSE 5

A   D A
If you get there before I do,

E
(Coming for to carry me home)

A   D A
Tell all my friends I'm coming too.

E   A
(Coming for to carry me home)

Repeat Chorus

THE KEY OF G

To play three-chord songs in the key of G, we need two new chords: G and C, as well as the D major chord. Let's start with the easier of these two chords, the C chord.

THE C CHORD

Note that the low E string is not played. Also, the G string is open, but the adjacent strings are fretted, so it is important to make sure that the G string is not accidentally muted by another finger. To check this, pick the strings one at a time while fretting the C chord, and listen to see whether they all sound. If an open string is accidentally muted, you will probably be able to feel it with the offending left-hand finger and adjust accordingly. This is excellent practice when learning any new chord.

THE G CHORD – TWO VERSIONS

The G chord can often be a challenge to begin with and it is one of those chords that different guitarists tend to have their own slightly different versions of. The first version here is probably the most commonly used. This can be a bit of a stretch, particularly for players with small hands. It's worth persevering with, because G major is a favourite key for guitar songs, and not just those with three-chords: four- and five-chord songs are also relatively easy.

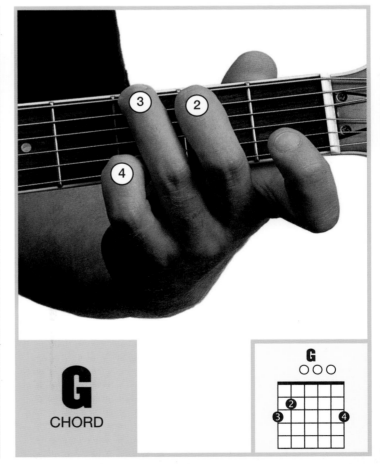

C CHORD

G CHORD

G ALT CHORD

This chord contains three open strings on the inside of the shape, so again it is important to make sure that these are not muted accidentally.

If you find this shape too challenging at first, you can use the alternative version (right). Some players use a different G chord shape as shown here. This is in some ways less of a stretch, though it can be a challenge as it uses all four fingers and it lends itself less well to changing to related chords. Because of the notes used, it sounds a little more 'rocky' than our basic version. It's a good idea to learn and practise both.

The following exercises use up to four chords found in the key of G major: G, C, D and Em. As usual, it's fine to start by strumming once, then twice, per bar before moving on to four strums, and at whatever tempo works for you.

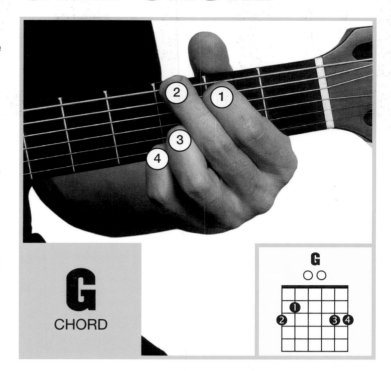

G
CHORD

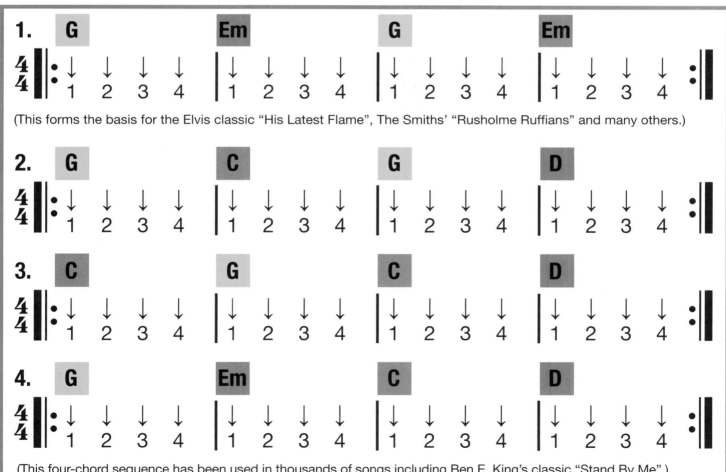

(This forms the basis for the Elvis classic "His Latest Flame", The Smiths' "Rusholme Ruffians" and many others.)

(This four-chord sequence has been used in thousands of songs including Ben E. King's classic "Stand By Me".)

Oh! Susanna

This classic song by Stephen Foster has been recorded by The Byrds and James Taylor. Our arrangement uses four chords in the key of G: G, Em, C and D.

CHORDS

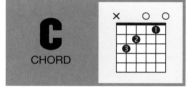

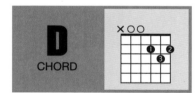

VERSE

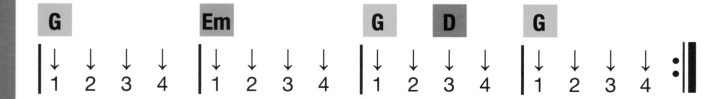

CHORUS

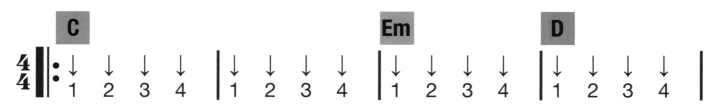

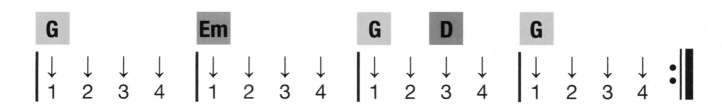

VERSE 1

G   Em D
I come from Alabama with my banjo on my knee,

G   Em   G   D G
I's gwine to Louisiana my own true love for to see.

G   Em   D
It rained all night the day I left, the weather it was dry;

G   Em   G D G
The sun so hot I froze to death – Susanna don't you cry.

CHORUS

C   G   D
Oh! Susanna don't you cry for me,

G   Em   G D G
I come from Alabama with my banjo on my knee.

VERSE 2

G   Em   D
I had a dream the other night when everything was still,

G   Em   G D G
I thought I saw Susanna dear, a-coming down the hill.

 G   Em   D
The buckwheat cake was in her mouth; a tear was in her eye,

G   Em   G D G
I says I'se coming from the South – Susanna don't you cry.

Repeat Chorus

THE Am CHORD

The Am chord looks exactly like the E chord, except that the whole shape is transferred to the adjacent set of strings. Only one finger is moved when changing from Am to C, so this is a natural and easy move defining the chord sequence of many popular songs, such as "House Of The Rising Sun".

Note that the low E string should not sound. Just as the chords E and Em have only one note that is different, so do the A and Am chords. This is the *third* of the chord, the note that defines the quality of the chord as major or minor.

GUITAR TIP: Try removing the first finger to let the open B string sound, and then adding it again on the next beat. This is another popular move like the D chord trick discussed on p. 30. The resulting chord is called Asus2.

Am
CHORD

Am

CHORD CHANGING EXERCISES

1. | Am | E | Am | G |

$\frac{4}{4}$ ‖: ↓ ↓ ↓ ↓ | ↓ ↓ ↓ ↓ | ↓ ↓ ↓ ↓ | ↓ ↓ ↓ ↓ :‖
  1 2 3 4 | 1 2 3 4 | 1 2 3 4 | 1 2 3 4

2. | Am | C | Am | E |

$\frac{4}{4}$ ‖: ↓ ↓ ↓ ↓ | ↓ ↓ ↓ ↓ | ↓ ↓ ↓ ↓ | ↓ ↓ ↓ ↓ :‖
  1 2 3 4 | 1 2 3 4 | 1 2 3 4 | 1 2 3 4

Notice that when changing between Am and C, only the third finger has to move – the others can stay in position.

3. | Am | G | D | C |

$\frac{4}{4}$ ‖: ↓ ↓ ↓ ↓ | ↓ ↓ ↓ ↓ | ↓ ↓ ↓ ↓ | ↓ ↓ ↓ ↓ :‖
  1 2 3 4 | 1 2 3 4 | 1 2 3 4 | 1 2 3 4

4. | Am | Em | G | E |

$\frac{4}{4}$ ‖: ↓ ↓ ↓ ↓ | ↓ ↓ ↓ ↓ | ↓ ↓ ↓ ↓ | ↓ ↓ ↓ ↓ :‖
  1 2 3 4 | 1 2 3 4 | 1 2 3 4 | 1 2 3 4

3. | Am | D | Am | G |

$\frac{4}{4}$ ‖: ↓ ↓ ↓ ↓ | ↓ ↓ ↓ ↓ | ↓ ↓ ↓ ↓ | ↓ ↓ ↓ ↓ :‖
  1 2 3 4 | 1 2 3 4 | 1 2 3 4 | 1 2 3 4

4. | Am | E | G | D |

$\frac{4}{4}$ ‖: ↓ ↓ ↓ ↓ | ↓ ↓ ↓ ↓ | ↓ ↓ ↓ ↓ | ↓ ↓ ↓ ↓ :‖
  1 2 3 4 | 1 2 3 4 | 1 2 3 4 | 1 2 3 4

CHANGING STRINGS

With time, guitar strings gradually corrode and begin to sound less bright and 'zingy'. Many professionals change their strings very often, but as a beginner you probably won't want to do it more than once every few months. Just like guitar playing, good results here require practice.

Ultimately, you will probably want to change all of the strings at once (unless you are replacing a broken string) but to begin with you may want to try changing one string at a time. This way no parts of the guitar can become detached, and you can check the other strings to see how the results of your work should look.

The fundamentals are the same for all guitars. Take a good look at your guitar before removing any strings to see exactly how they are attached.

EQUIPMENT

A winder/trimmer can be used for removing old strings, trimming new ones and quickly winding the new string on to the machinehead.

GUITAR STRINGS

It is crucial to get the right strings for your guitar. In particular, using steel strings on a classical guitar can result in irreparable damage to the neck and bridge. There are three main types of string sets:

Electric guitar strings: These generally have three wound strings (E A D) and three plain strings (G B E). The wound strings are usually the same colour as the plain strings (nickel).

Acoustic steel strings: These look a lot like electric guitar strings except that the third (G) string is generally wound, and the winding is usually an alloy containing bronze.

Classical (nylon) strings: The top three strings are made from solid nylon. The bottom three strings are made of many strands of very fine nylon, with a soft metal winding – this is usually silver in colour.

String Winder

Removing Strings
Using a trimmer/winder tool to lever a bridge pin out before removing a string.

Pin

REMOVING THE OLD STRING

Slacken the string and then cut it anywhere between the bridge and the nut. You may need to use your trimmer to disentangle the string from the machinehead. On an acoustic guitar, you will need to remove the bridge pin. Avoid using pliers, as you can easily damage the surface of the bridge. The safest method is to push the pin out from inside the guitar using a hard object such as a coin (slacken the rest of the strings first in order to get your hand in through the sound hole).

ATTACHING THE NEW STRING ON AN ACOUSTIC GUITAR

The new string should be attached at the bridge first. On a standard acoustic guitar, simply feed the ball end of the string in through the hole in the bridge, place the pin loosely back in the hole, pull the string so that the ball makes contact with the end of the pin, and then push the pin firmly into the hole.

Nut

Tuning Peg

Headstock   **Machinehead**

Classical Strings
A classical guitar headstock. Changing classical strings can be a little more difficult than acoustic or electric strings.

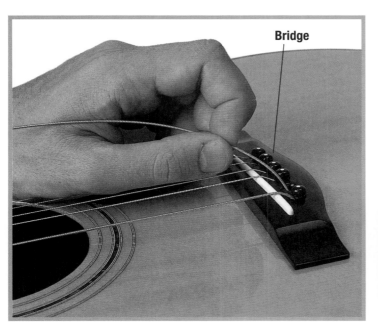

Bridge

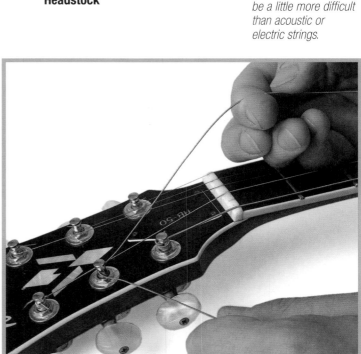

ATTACHING THE NEW STRING ON AN ELECTRIC GUITAR

On most electric guitars, attachment to the bridge is very simple, and you should be able to see exactly where to thread the string by looking at the others. On most Fender guitars, the strings pass through the body, so the string should be fed through from the back.

ATTACHING THE NEW STRING ON A CLASSICAL GUITAR

Classical guitar strings are wrapped around the bridge in a complex kind of knot. Classical strings do not have ball ends, so the string can be fed through the bridge from the sound hole side, looped under itself and then wrapped around itself on the top surface of the bridge.

Most guitars are essentially the same at the headstock. The string should be fed through the hole in the machinehead so that it can be wound around it about five times. Plain strings can be looped through again before winding. Make a sharp kink in the string on the other side of the hole before winding the string to full tension, using a string winder if you have one.

Finally, tug the string away from the body a few times to stretch it and take up any slack – this greatly reduces the amount of time it takes to 'play in' the string (when it will tend to go flat quickly as you play it). Tune the string as normal using a tuner. Don't forget that the other strings will almost certainly also need retuning at this point.

PLAY A SONG

The Water Is Wide

This traditional English song remains popular today and has been recorded by artists as diverse as Eva Cassidy, Neil Young and James Taylor. Our arrangement in the key of G uses five chords: G, Em, Am, C and D.

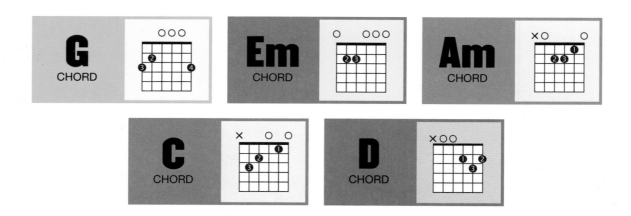

VERSE

G				C				G							
↓	↓	↓	↓	↓	↓	↓	↓	↓	↓	↓	↓	↓	↓	↓	↓
1	2	3	4	1	2	3	4	1	2	3	4	1	2	3	4

Em				C				D							
↓	↓	↓	↓	↓	↓	↓	↓	↓	↓	↓	↓	↓	↓	↓	↓
1	2	3	4	1	2	3	4	1	2	3	4	1	2	3	4

CHORUS

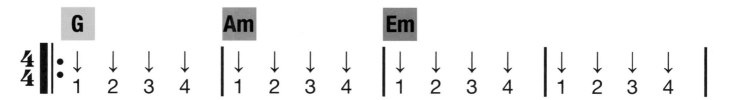

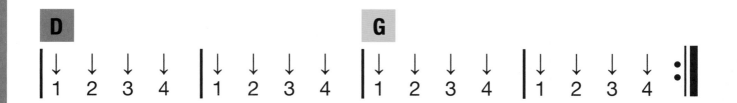

VERSE 1

G   C   G
The water is wide,   I can't cross over,
Em   C   D
And neither have I wings to fly.
G   Am   Em
Build me a boat   that will carry two,
D   G
And both shall row, my love and I.

VERSE 2

G   C   G
There is a ship,   and she sails the sea,
Em   C   D
She's loaded deep,   as deep can be.
G   Am   Em
But not so deep   as the love I'm in,
D   G
I know not how I sink or swim.

VERSE 3

G   C   G
Oh love is handsome   and love is fine,
Em   C   D
The sweetest flower   when it's first new.
G   Am   Em
But love grows old   and waxes cold
D   G
And fades away like summer dew.

ED SHEERAN
1991–

Ed Sheeran may well turn out to be one of the most successful singer-songwriters of the second decade of the twenty-first century. His debut album +, released in 2011, has achieved multi-platinum status and a number one position in charts across the world. Before being signed to a major record label, Sheeran had made a string of self-released EPs over a five-year period that also included an intensive live performance schedule; in one year alone, Ed Sheeran clocked up over 300 live appearances. This period also saw collaborations and tours with other more established acts, including the *No. 5 Collaborations* EP that featured a number of acts prominent in the 'grime' genre.

Sheeran's songs are often powerful and personal, and produced in a folk-pop British style with roots going back to Van Morrison via recent influences such as Damien Rice and James Morrison. Perhaps his most successful song, "Lego House" uses carefully layered acoustic and electric guitars; the main electric guitar figure makes clever use of delays to produce a subtly propulsive rhythmic figure.

Sheeran's acoustic guitar style varies from simple fingerpicking accompaniment to much more complex layered effects; for live performance he often uses a looper pedal (a kind of delay pedal that can keep repeating a musical phrase) to create a 'multi-tracked'

Little Martin
Ed Sheeran favours the surprisingly big sound of this conveniently small guitar.

accompaniment incorporating elements of percussion produced by hammering on the guitar body and slapping the strings.

Sheeran has collaborated with major international artists including Taylor Swift (the song "Everything Has Changed" from *Red*) and One Direction (two songs on their second album *Take Me Home*).

FAVOURED GUITARS:

MARTIN LITTLE MARTIN LX1E

CHAPTER 3:
EXPLORING RHYTHMS

Rhythm is often called the most important element in music as it is the defining aspect of many musical styles. A little rhythmic knowledge goes a long way on the guitar.

LEFT: Bob Marley and the Wailers

UPSTROKES

So far we have been strumming in one direction only: downwards, once per beat or less. Many guitar styles involve strumming between the beats too. Sometimes, these can also be downstrokes, but since you have to move the hand upwards for each of these, it often makes sense to use the upward motion to play the strings too.

Alternating Strokes
In many medium-tempo styles, the right hand strums downwards on the beat and upwards on the offbeat.

Upstroke
Here the right hand moves upwards. Usually upstrokes are a little lighter than downstrokes and may not catch all the strings.

50

PREPARATION – COUNTING OFFBEATS

Strums or notes occurring between beats are called offbeats. To understand these, start by counting '1, 2, 3, 4' in time with a metronome or other regular pulse. Next, add an 'and' between the beats:

'1 & 2 & 3 & 4 & 1 & 2 & 3 & 4 &'

The offbeats should fall exactly halfway between the beats. Once this seems natural, do the same thing on the guitar. Start by strumming any chord on every beat, then add upstrokes for the offbeats.

MIXED PATTERNS

Often, guitar strumming patterns include some, but not all of the offbeats. If we are using upstrokes for offbeats, this should remain consistent, and downstrokes should always be used on the beat. Missing out some of the offbeats will therefore still involve performing an upstroke, but one where you miss the strings rather than playing them. This is called a phantom or ghost stroke.

Practise the following strumming patterns, remembering that downstrokes should always fall on the beat, and upstrokes should be on the offbeat – whether they are heard or phantom strokes.

REGGAE

In the reggae music style, rhythm guitar parts often use upstrokes almost exclusively. Full shapes such as those we have seen so far are rarely used, however; try playing the top (highest) three strings of the chords you know on offbeats only, for a flavour of this.

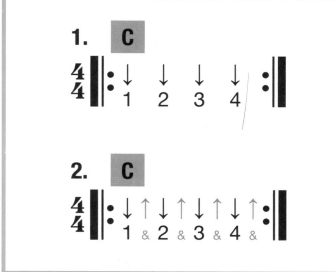

EXERCISES

These exercises combine all of the chords learned so far with many possible rhythms using downstrokes and upstrokes. For now at least, downstrokes should always be used on the beat, and upstrokes on the offbeat. To help you maintain focus on changing chords, the strumming rhythm will be the same for the duration of each exercise.

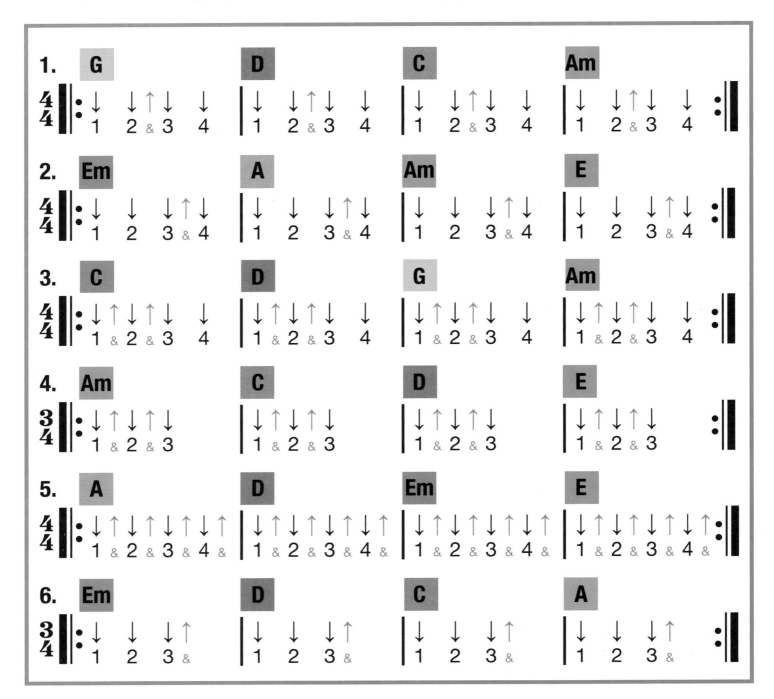

BUILDING A CHORD

The shapes we have learned so far form the basis of many simple guitar accompaniments, but it can also be useful to be able to construct chords yourself. If you know the names of all the notes in the first four frets, and the notes needed to build a range of chords, you can try finding chords yourself.

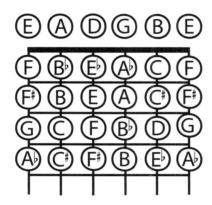

The diagram above shows all the notes in the first four frets. The notes A, B, C, D, E, F and G are called natural notes – these are the white notes on a piano. The notes in between, or black notes, are called sharps and flats. Each of these actually has two possible names; we have shown the commonest name for each for the sake of simplicity.

However, you will also need to know the alternative names:

F♯ (F sharp) = G♭ (G flat)

A♭ (A flat) = G♯ (G sharp)

B♭ (B flat) = A♯ (A sharp)

C♯ (C sharp) = D♭ (D flat)

E♭ (E flat) = D♯ (D sharp)

CHORD SPELLINGS

To make a major or minor chord, three different notes need to appear at least once: the root, third and fifth. As the guitar has six strings, there may be more than one occurrence of some of these. Usually, the root note should be placed on the lowest sounding string.

	Major			Minor		
	Root	Third	Fifth	Root	Third	Fifth
C	C	E	G	C	E♭	G
D	D	F♯	A	D	F	A
E	E	G♯	B	E	G	B
F	F	A	C	F	A♭	C
G	G	B	D	G	B♭	D
A	A	C♯	E	A	C	E
B	B	D♯	F♯	B	D	F♯

Beautiful Dreamer

This 'parlor song' by Stephen Foster is a beautiful song with a melody that lends itself to any number of styles – it was even a staple of The Beatles' early live sets in a raucous rock 'n' roll version. Our version in $\frac{3}{4}$ time is closer to the original and should be played at a suitably dreamy tempo.

CHORDS

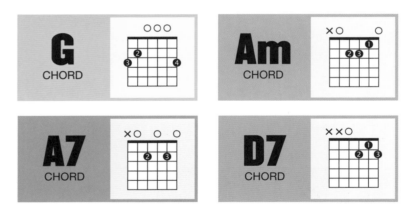

VERSE

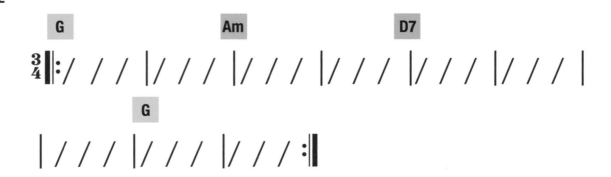

CHORUS

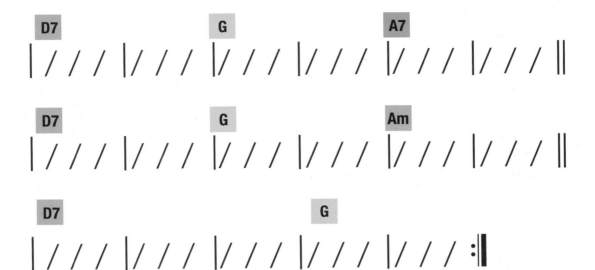

VERSE 1

G   **Am**
Beautiful dreamer, wake unto me,

D7   **G**
Starlight and dewdrops are awaiting thee.

                         Am
Sounds of the rude world heard in the day,

D7   **G**
Led by the moonlight have all passed away.

D7   **G**
Beautiful dreamer, queen of my song,

A7   **D7**
List while I woo thee with soft melody.

G   **Am**
Gone are the cares of life's busy throng,

D7   **G**
Beautiful dreamer awake unto me.

VERSE 2

G   **Am**
Beautiful dreamer, out on the sea,

D7   **G**
Mermaids are chanting the wild Lorelei,

                         Am
Over the streamlet vapors are borne,

D7   **G**
Waiting to fade at the bright coming morn.

D7   **G**
Beautiful dreamer, beam on my heart,

A7   **D7**
E'en as the morn on the streamlet and sea,

G   **Am**
Then will all clouds of sorrow depart,

D7   **G**
Beautiful dreamer awake unto me,

D7   **G**
Beautiful dreamer awake unto me.

JOHN MAYER
1977–

RECOMMENDED LISTENING:
Room For Squares (album)
Continuum (album)
Paradise Valley (album)

John Mayer has explored a broad range of musical styles in his career, moving from acoustic-driven folky pop to a hard-edged blues style noticeably influenced by Jimi Hendrix and Stevie Ray Vaughan.

Like many of his generation, the young Mayer developed a fascination for the electric guitar after watching Michael J. Fox's mimed rendition of Chuck Berry's "Johnny B. Goode" as Marty McFly in *Back to the Future*, which led him to explore blues-derived styles and the music of Stevie Ray Vaughan in particular. He later spent two semesters studying at Berklee College of Music before leaving to pursue non-musical studies.

Mayer was an early pioneer of the possibilities of digital distribution, initially releasing his first album *Room For Squares* on the internet only before signing a deal with Columbia Records, who remixed the album for physical release. This album produced several major hits including "Your Body Is A Wonderland".

During the next few years, Mayer moved ever closer towards a blues style, initially in the live arena with his John Mayer Trio – the classic blues/rock power trio line-up of guitar, bass and drums. This blues direction has led to notable collaborations with giants of the style including B.B. King, Buddy Guy and Eric Clapton.

Mayer has collaborated with several companies who have produced John Mayer 'signature' guitars and custom designed amplifiers. His personal guitar collection, estimated to number over 200 instruments, reflects these collaborations.

OMJM John Mayer
John Mayer has worked with designers from several guitar and amp manufacturers to create custom models, including Martin and Fender.

FAVOURED GUITARS:

**FENDER JOHN
MAYER SIGNATURE
STRATOCASTER
MARTIN OM-28 JOHN
MAYER ACOUSTIC**

CHAPTER 4:
GETTING BLUESY

Most popular music is descended in one way or another from the blues – the dominant Afro-American style of the early twentieth century.

LEFT: Muddy Waters

INTRODUCING B7

Our next chord is a little more challenging. It's more complex in several ways: its name, sound and the use of all four fingers. The B7 chord sounds more complex because it contains more different notes than the major and minor chords we have seen so far. Seventh chords are commonly found in the blues, and other styles derived from the blues including jazz and rock.

Using all four fingers means that there is more chance of accidentally muting notes if the fingers are not placed accurately. Again, check that all notes of the chord are sounding clearly by playing them one at a time (apart from the low E string, which is not played). If any note is not sounding properly, it may be that you are applying insufficient finger pressure, or the finger is not close enough to the fret. If another finger is accidentally muting the string, you will probably feel it in that finger when you pluck the string.

B7
CHORD

TRY B7

B7 is found in several popular keys on the guitar, including E major and E minor. The following exercises will help you practise changing to and from B7 in these keys and typical chord sequences in other keys.

EXERCISES

Chord charts are often written without specific rhythms. 'Real world' chord charts often show just the time signature barlines, with four slashes (if we are in 4/4) to represent the beats in each bar. The exact rhythms used, and other stylistic issues, are decided by the individual musician.

For these exercises, try to make up your own rhythms or use rhythms from previous exercises. As before, maintain one rhythm for the duration of the exercise; this will help you maintain focus on the changing chords in time. Don't forget, if you are finding this challenging, you can let each chord ring for a whole bar, before progressing to two strums per chord, then one strum and finally more developed rhythms using upstrokes.

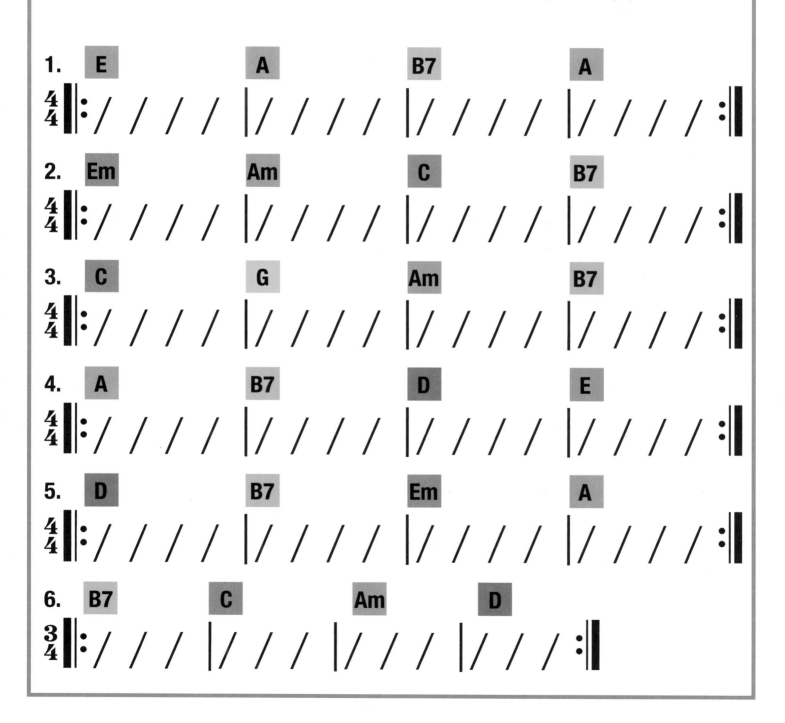

MORE SEVENTH CHORDS

Any major chord can be turned into a seventh chord. On the guitar, this often involves changing just one note in a major shape, so seventh chords can be easy to remember, though this sometimes results in fretting the other notes with different fingers. The commonest seventh chords are shown by simply adding '7' after the name of the root note.

In the E7 and A7 shapes below, the change is very simple: one fretted note is removed; the extra note is an open string. For E7, the rest of the fingers are unaffected; you could take this approach to A7 too, but most players use fingers 2 and 3 as it's a bit more comfortable.

For the D7 chord, the seventh is a fretted note, which means that different fingers have to be used to play the other notes.

E7 CHORD

E7
× O O O

A7 CHORD

A7
× O O O

D7 CHORD

D7

× × ○

PRACTICE CHORD SEQUENCES

Seventh chords belong naturally as the fifth chord in a major or minor key (known as chord V or the dominant seventh). The seventh chords we have learned so far belong in the following easy keys in this context:

Key	Dominant Chord
G	D7
E/Em	B7
A/Am	E7
D	A7

Let's put some seventh chords into 3- and 4-chord practice sequences.

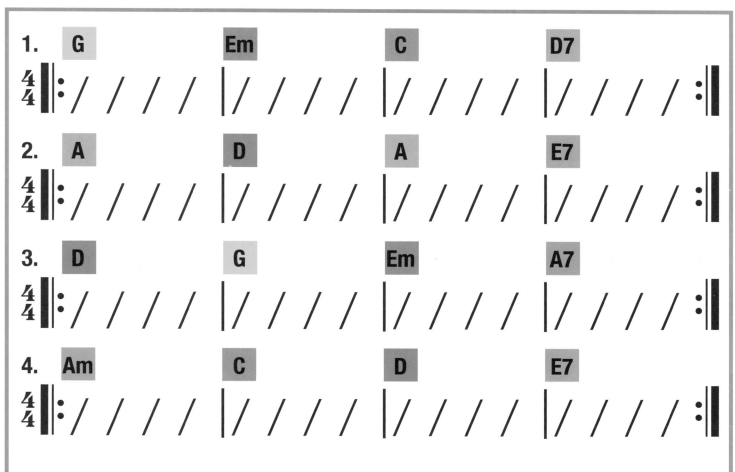

PLAY A SONG

Aura Lea

This song from the American Civil War song was recorded by Burl Ives; the melody achieved greater fame as adapted by Elvis Presley with new lyrics in the song "Love Me Tender". All the seventh chords introduced in this chapter are used in this song.

CHORDS

CHORD SEQUENCE

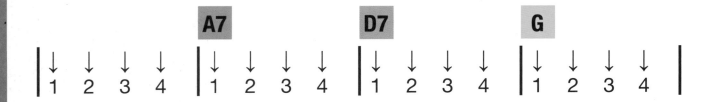

A

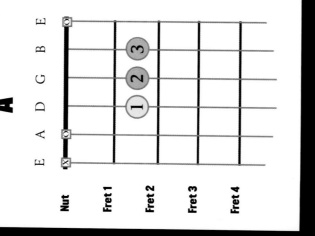

A7

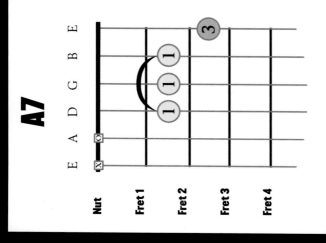

Am

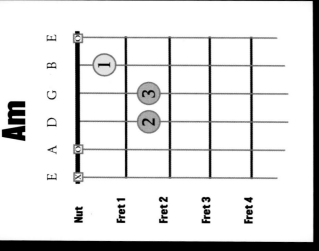

B

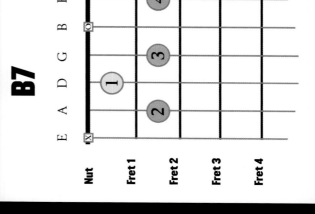

B7

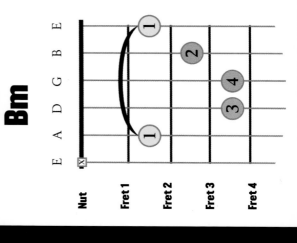

Bm

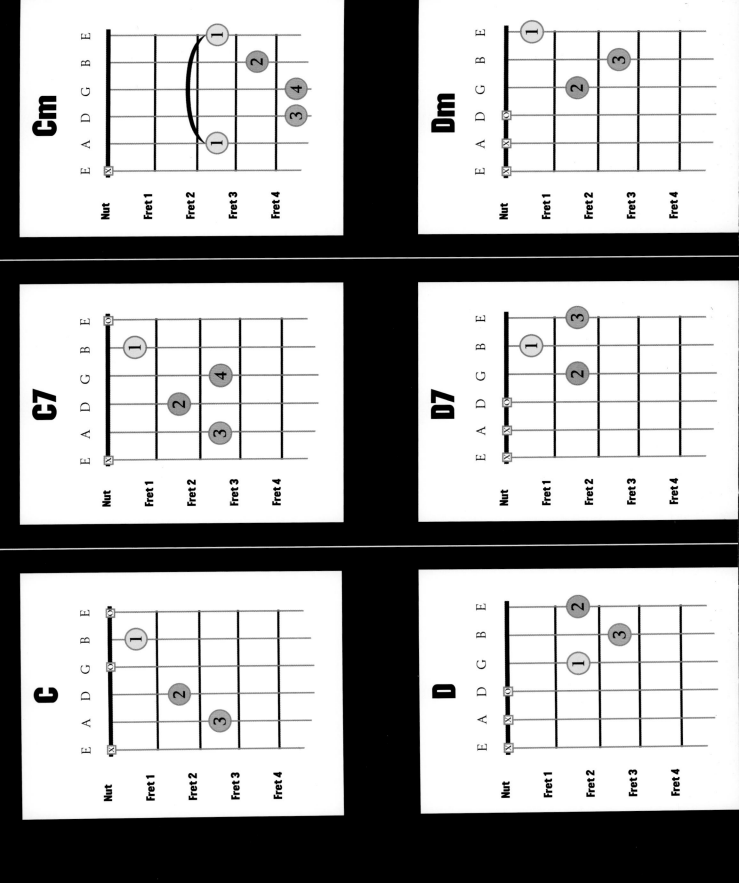

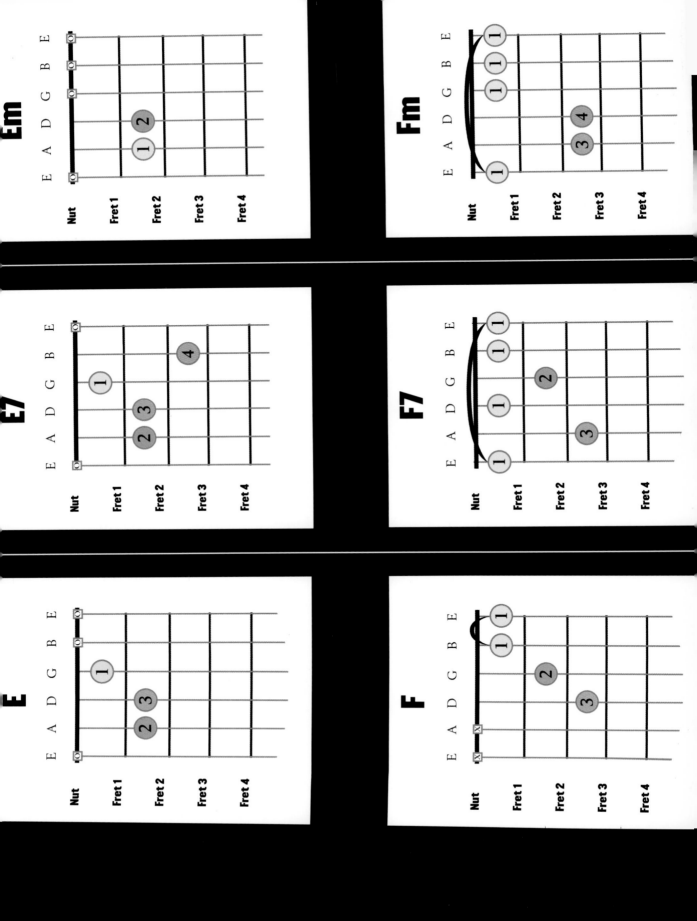

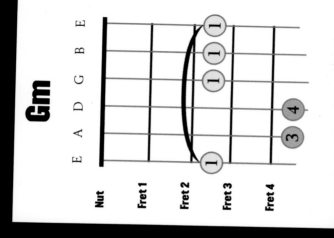

Gm

E A D G B E

Nut
Fret 1
Fret 2
Fret 3
Fret 4

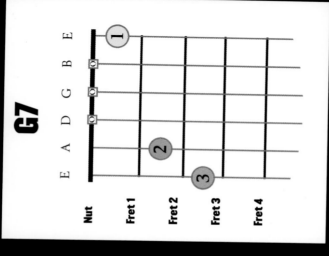

G7

E A D G B E

Nut
Fret 1
Fret 2
Fret 3
Fret 4

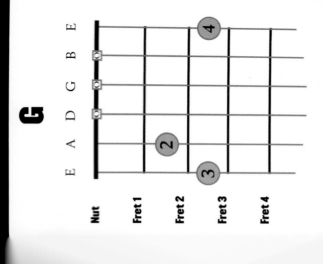

G

E A D G B E

Nut
Fret 1
Fret 2
Fret 3
Fret 4

MAJOR CHORDS

Major chords are probably the most frequently used chords in all Western music. In a major key, major chords can be built on the first, fourth and fifth steps of the scale. These are called the primary chords. Thousands of songs in a huge variety of styles can be played using just these three chords, for example G, C and D (I, IV and V) in the key of G major.

SEVENTH CHORDS

'7' chords, also known as dominant seventh chords, are formed by adding a minor or flattened seventh to a major chord. This occurs within the major key on the fifth ('dominant') step of the scale; when other chords in the key have a flattened seventh this tends to give them a bluesy sound. Dominant sevenths are used all over blues, rock and jazz, for example a twelve bar blues in the key of G usually contains the chords G7, C7 and D7 (I7, IV7 and V7).

MINOR CHORDS

Minor chords are often described as sad compared to major chords. Alongside the primary chords, there are also three minor chords in the major key. These are known as secondary chords and are found on the second, third and sixth steps. For example, you can play many four-chord songs in G major using G, C, D and Em (I, IV, V and vi*). *In this notation, major chords are usually indicated using upper case roman numerals while minor chords use lower case.

① = First finger
② = Second finger
③ = Third finger
④ = Fourth finger
○ = Open string
☒ = Do not play this string

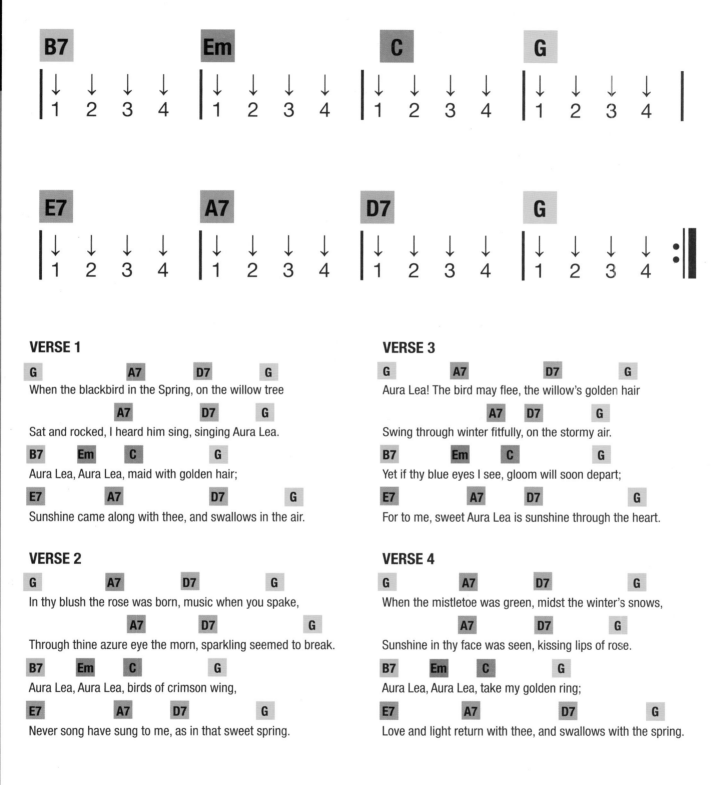

VERSE 1

G   A7 D7 G

When the blackbird in the Spring, on the willow tree

A7 D7 G

Sat and rocked, I heard him sing, singing Aura Lea.

B7 Em C   G

Aura Lea, Aura Lea, maid with golden hair;

E7   A7   D7   G

Sunshine came along with thee, and swallows in the air.

VERSE 2

G A7 D7   G

In thy blush the rose was born, music when you spake,

A7 D7   G

Through thine azure eye the morn, sparkling seemed to break.

B7 Em C   G

Aura Lea, Aura Lea, birds of crimson wing,

E7   A7 D7   G

Never song have sung to me, as in that sweet spring.

VERSE 3

G   A7 D7 G

Aura Lea! The bird may flee, the willow's golden hair

A7 D7 G

Swing through winter fitfully, on the stormy air.

B7 Em C   G

Yet if thy blue eyes I see, gloom will soon depart;

E7   A7 D7   G

For to me, sweet Aura Lea is sunshine through the heart.

VERSE 4

G A7 D7   G

When the mistletoe was green, midst the winter's snows,

A7 D7   G

Sunshine in thy face was seen, kissing lips of rose.

B7 Em C   G

Aura Lea, Aura Lea, take my golden ring;

E7   A7   D7   G

Love and light return with thee, and swallows with the spring.

THE TWELVE BAR BLUES

The origins of this three-chord song structure are lost in the mists of time; it is likely that it originated at least 150 years ago. It is probably the most commonly used chord sequence in history – certainly in a lot of popular music. Possibly because so many songs use this sequence, it always feels completely 'right' – and not just for songs that start with 'I woke up this morning…'.

As its name suggests, this twelve bar sequence is central to the music known as the blues, but has also formed the basis of a substantial proportion of rock, pop and jazz – in the latter case, often in more advanced versions employing far more than three chords.

In its basic form, the twelve-bar sequence is found in hundreds of blues and rock 'n' roll classics. Once you have the measure of the sequence, you can try any of these songs yourself.

Seventh chords have a fundamentally 'bluesy' character and can be used for any of the three chords in this sequence, but in some styles simpler major chords are used. So in the exercises below you can play E anywhere you see E7, for example.

TRY THESE BLUES SONGS...

If you know any of these songs, try singing them along to the twelve-bar sequence below: they will all work…

"Kansas City"   "Twenty Flight Rock"

"Sweet Home Chicago"   "Johnny B. Goode"

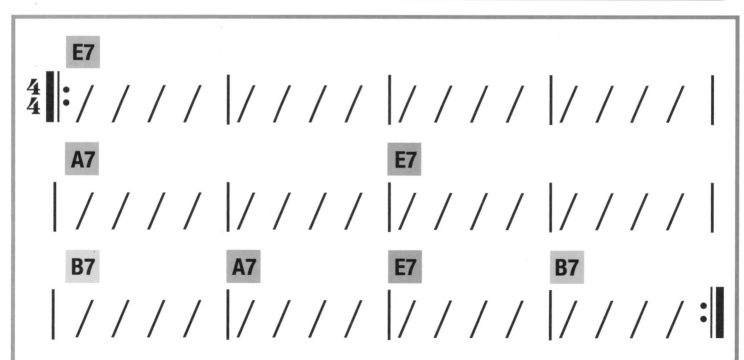

THE ORIGINS OF THE BLUES

The essential character of the blues is a result of a musical culture clash – between European harmony and African melody. It is likely that Afro-American slaves would sing while they worked in order to add a rhythmic structure to burdensome and boring manual labour. For some reason the minor pentatonic scale is used in this role across the world – you hear it in simple playground chants, and also among marching soldiers ('I don't know but I've been told…').

Singing minor pentatonic melodies over chord sequences using major chords results in some notes that clash. These are known as blue notes. In the earliest blues recordings, this is really noticeable, creating a plaintive quality perfect for any tale of woe. As the style developed, the blue notes began to be incorporated into the harmony: this is why almost all blues sequences use seventh chords rather than simple major chords. This reduces the clashing effect while also creating a harmonic language unique to the blues and derived forms.

NATIONAL RESONATOR

Before the invention of the electric guitar, guitar players often found that they simply didn't have the volume to compete with louder instruments such as drums and horns. Various attempts were made to boost the guitar's volume, including the resonator guitar. This uses one or more aluminium cones built into the body of the instrument, which act like as loudspeakers amplifying vibrations straight from the strings. The increase in volume is not spectacular, but the resulting slightly nasal tone is very distinctive, and perfect for various styles of American music including blues and country.

National Resonator Guitar

These instruments were immortalized in Paul Simon's lyric "The Mississippi Delta was shining like a National guitar…"

MINOR PENTATONIC SCALE

This is the minor pentatonic scale. Try playing this, from the lowest sounding note to the highest, for a flavour of the early blues sound. The notes marked 'R' show the tonic note or key note. To find this scale in A, the lowest 'R' (on the low E string) should be at the fifth fret.

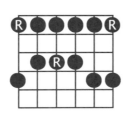

Ⓡ = Root

THE FLATTENED FIFTH

The minor pentatonic contains two 'blue notes' in relation to the major key. Adding a third blue note, the flattened fifth, results in the scale commonly known as the blues scale. This is commonly used in blues, jazz and rock wherever a bluesy feel is called for.

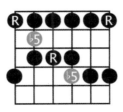

Ⓡ = Root

♭5 = Flattened Fifth

USING A CAPO

The capo is a really handy device that makes it possible to play in different keys without learning new chord shapes, by effectively shortening the guitar's scale length and strings. There are many different types of capo – most use either some form of spring tension or elastic to stay in place and push the strings down.

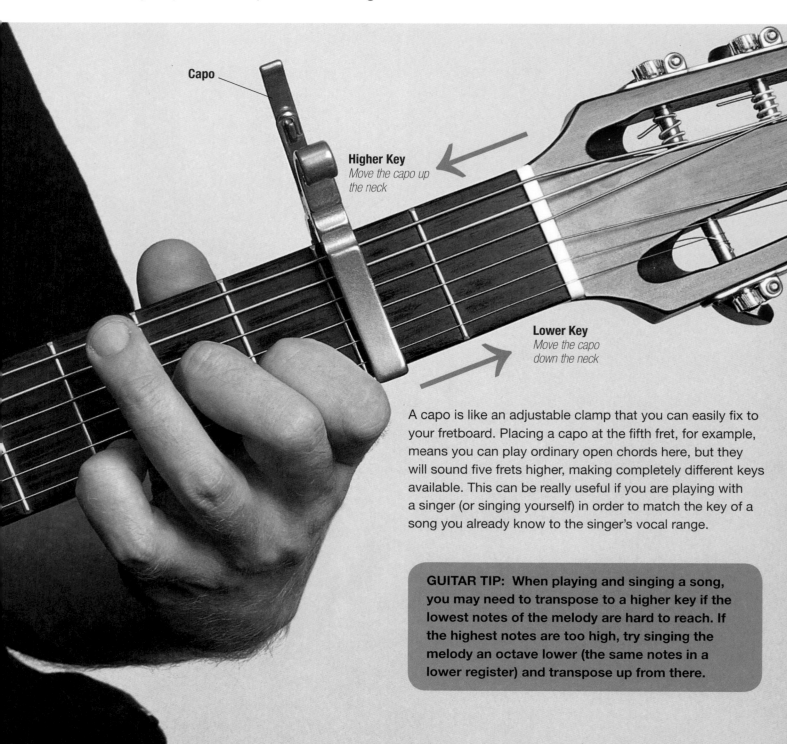

Capo

Higher Key
Move the capo up the neck

Lower Key
Move the capo down the neck

A capo is like an adjustable clamp that you can easily fix to your fretboard. Placing a capo at the fifth fret, for example, means you can play ordinary open chords here, but they will sound five frets higher, making completely different keys available. This can be really useful if you are playing with a singer (or singing yourself) in order to match the key of a song you already know to the singer's vocal range.

GUITAR TIP: When playing and singing a song, you may need to transpose to a higher key if the lowest notes of the melody are hard to reach. If the highest notes are too high, try singing the melody an octave lower (the same notes in a lower register) and transpose up from there.

CHOOSING A CAPO

When choosing a capo, the most important thing is to check whether your guitar has a flat fretboard or a curved one. Capos are designed to match this and using the wrong type may result in buzzing or muted strings.

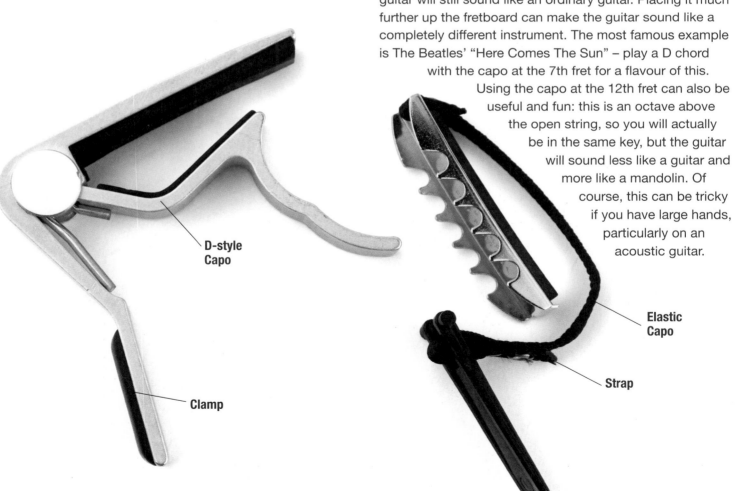

D-style Capo

Clamp

USING A CAPO FOR EFFECT

Using the capo on the lower frets can be useful, but the guitar will still sound like an ordinary guitar. Placing it much further up the fretboard can make the guitar sound like a completely different instrument. The most famous example is The Beatles' "Here Comes The Sun" – play a D chord with the capo at the 7th fret for a flavour of this. Using the capo at the 12th fret can also be useful and fun: this is an octave above the open string, so you will actually be in the same key, but the guitar will sound less like a guitar and more like a mandolin. Of course, this can be tricky if you have large hands, particularly on an acoustic guitar.

Elastic Capo

Strap

CHAPTER 5:

BARRE CHORDS

These chords may present a challenge at first, but they are essential tools for many players, allowing them to play in any key with ease.

LEFT: Danielle Haim from Haim

BARRE CHORDS

You might think that moving a basic chord shape further up the neck would be an easy way to generate new chords and play in different keys. Actually it is, but the important thing is that the open strings must be transposed too. If you were to move only the fretted notes (of an E chord, for example), these would no longer maintain the same relationship with the open strings, which would result in very different (and not generally useable) chords. So we need a way to move the open strings too.

WHAT IS A BARRE?

Using the index finger almost like a capo. If we place the index finger across (usually) all six strings at a given fret and press down, they will all be transposed together. This technique is called a *barre*. If we move the E chord up a fret it becomes an F, then F sharp, G, A flat and so on.

F CHORD

Fm CHORD

One of the most useful barre chords is based on the E major chord shape. Transposing this up by one fret, using a barre at the first fret, results in an F major chord.

Removing the second finger from this shape results in an Fm chord (Em transposed up one fret).

Barre chords can be tough for a beginner to master; it may take some time to develop the necessary finger strength. Even for more experienced players, using barre chords for a whole song can cause some strain. However, they can work well when mixed with easier chords too. The following exercises integrate the F and Fm chords into sequences using familiar chords.

EXERCISES

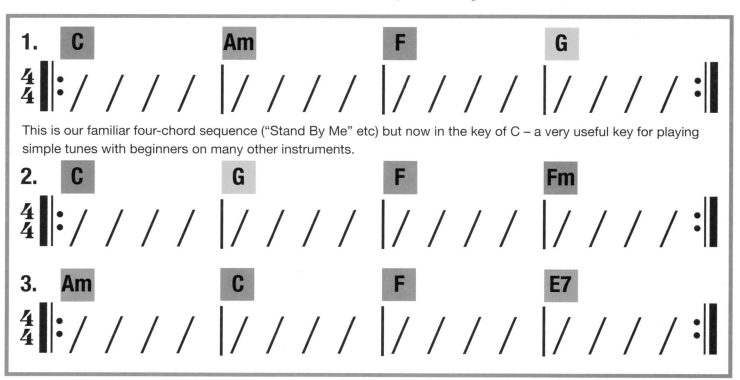

1. C   Am   F   G

This is our familiar four-chord sequence ("Stand By Me" etc) but now in the key of C – a very useful key for playing simple tunes with beginners on many other instruments.

2. C   G   F   Fm

3. Am   C   F   E7

MORE BARRE CHORDS

Many other shapes can be transposed using barre chords. The Am shape is very useful, opening up more advanced chord sequences in familiar keys. It's also almost the same physical shape as the E-based barre chord, so taking it up the fretboard should present no additional difficulties. Although this is essentially a full barre chord, the low E string is not played with this shape.

Using a barre at the second fret to transpose the Am chord up by a whole tone results in the very useful Bm chord.

Bm
CHORD

GUITAR TIP: When moving a shape up the fretboard, the fretboard dots can be a very useful navigational tool. They are usually placed at the 3rd, 5th, 7th, 9th and 12th fret (and beyond this, depending on how many frets your guitar has). Moving the Am-based barre shape to these frets results in Cm, Dm, Em, F#m and Am.

GUITAR TIP: Many of the frets where there are markers are associated with *harmonics*. These are bell-like notes produced by touching the string very lightly at a precise point rather than pushing it down on to the fretboard (and picking as usual). The easiest harmonics to play are found directly above the 12th, 7th and 5th frets.

EXERCISES

These exercises use just one barre chord (Bm) combined with familiar first position chords.

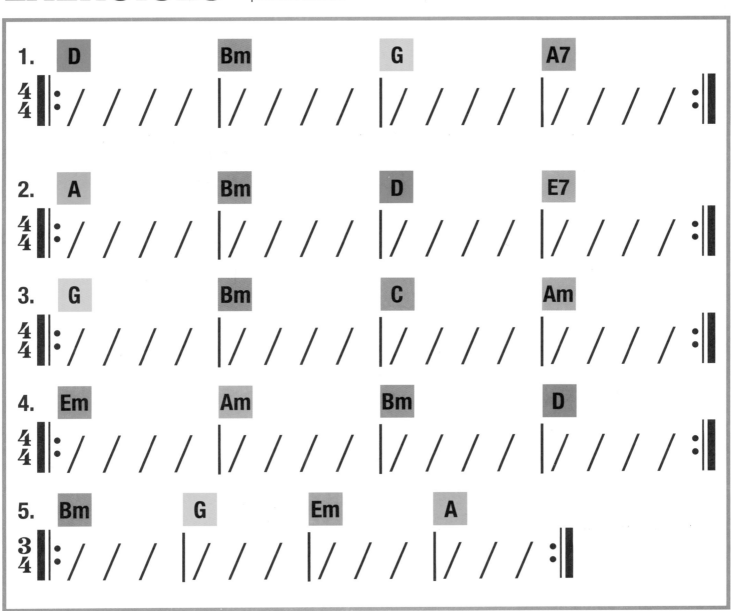

PLAY A SONG

House Of The Rising Sun

This American folk song was a massive hit for The Animals, but has also been recorded by Dolly Parton and Nina Simone among others. The song is in waltz time, written here as $\frac{3}{4}$. The arrangement here uses a simple but propulsive strumming pattern; later, you could try it with the fingerpicking patterns shown on p. 103 to get closer to The Animals' version.

CHORDS

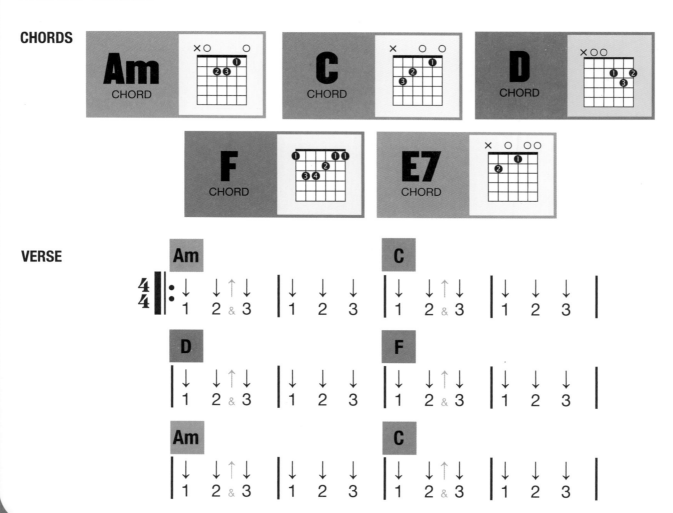

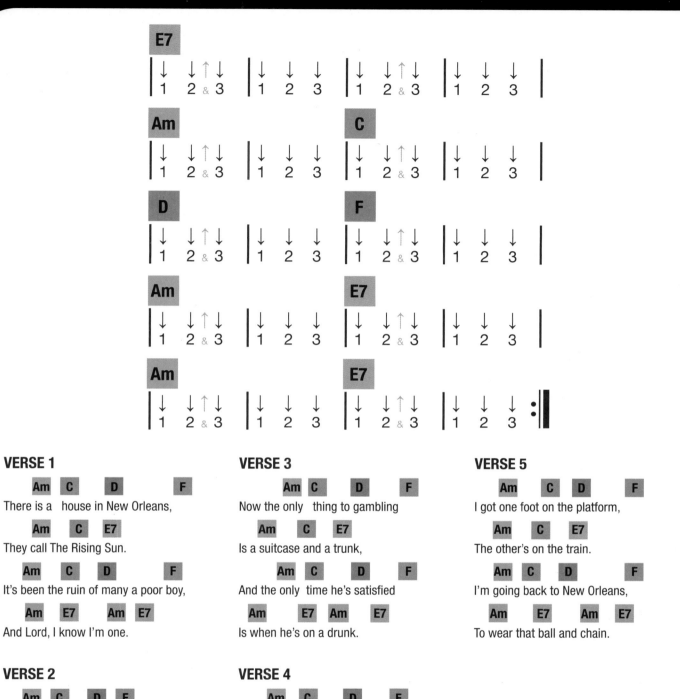

VERSE 1

`Am` `C`   `D`   `F`

There is a house in New Orleans,

`Am`   `C`   `E7`

They call The Rising Sun.

`Am`   `C`   `D`   `F`

It's been the ruin of many a poor boy,

`Am`   `E7`   `Am` `E7`

And Lord, I know I'm one.

VERSE 2

`Am` `C`   `D` `F`

My mother was a tailor,

`Am`   `C`   `E7`

She sewed my new blue jeans.

`Am` `C` `D`   `F`

My father was a gamblin' man,

`Am`   `E7` `Am`   `E7`

Down in New Orleans.

VERSE 3

`Am` `C`   `D`   `F`

Now the only thing to gambling

`Am`   `C`   `E7`

Is a suitcase and a trunk,

`Am` `C`   `D`   `F`

And the only time he's satisfied

`Am`   `E7` `Am`   `E7`

Is when he's on a drunk.

VERSE 4

`Am` `C`   `D`   `F`

Now mother, tell your children

`Am`   `C`   `E7`

Not to do what I have done,

`Am`   `C`   `D`   `F`

Spend your lives in sin and misery

`Am`   `E7` `Am` `E7`

In the House Of The Rising Sun

VERSE 5

`Am`   `C` `D`   `F`

I got one foot on the platform,

`Am`   `C`   `E7`

The other's on the train.

`Am` `C`   `D`   `F`

I'm going back to New Orleans,

`Am`   `E7`   `Am` `E7`

To wear that ball and chain.

PASSENGER
1984–

RECOMMENDED LISTENING:
Divers & Submarines (album)
Flight Of The Crow (album)
All The Little Lights (album)

Passenger is the stage name of Mike Rosenberg, a British singer-songwriter and guitarist. Passenger originated as a band, releasing one album before splitting; Rosenberg decided to continue with the name as a solo artist, initially as a busker. This took him to Australia where he forged links with Australian acts including John Butler, with whom he later toured the UK.

Passenger's huge international breakthrough came with his third album *All The Little Lights*, and in particular the single "Let Her Go", both of which achieved multi-platinum sales and number one chart positions across the world. An ongoing association with fellow British singer-songwriter Ed Sheeran, with whom Passenger has toured regularly, helped achieve this.

Passenger's style has been compared with David Gray and Cat Stevens, among others. His songs are instantly identifiable as a result of his light, distinctive voice and challenging, often humorous lyrics. On the guitar, he employs a simple style of acoustic accompaniment, using both strumming and fingerpicking. His technique falls in the tradition of fingerpicking singer-songwriters such as Paul Simon, often employing the semi-classical technique of arpeggiation with a continuous thumb bass line. His more up-tempo strummed accompaniments are generally played with high energy – an important factor for a busker

Gibson J-45
Like many singer-songwriters who started out as buskers, Passenger favours acoustic guitars with a loud and clear sound, such as the classic Gibson J-45.

when trying to grab the attention of anyone passing. Passenger's live set incorporates many covers, from both obvious and less obvious sources (including Simon & Garfunkel's "The Sound Of Silence", Bruce Springsteen's "Dancing In The Dark" and Survivor's "Eye Of The Tiger" as an introduction to his own huge hit "Let Her Go").

FAVOURED GUITAR:

GIBSON J-45

SYNCOPATION

Strumming downstrokes and upstrokes can be used to play some fairly complex patterns. Just as we can miss the strings on some of the upstrokes, we can also miss the strings on one or more downstrokes in the bar (phantom downstrokes). This produces an effect known as syncopation, where the offbeats are emphasized more than usual.

To produce one of the most useful syncopated strumming patterns, start with this rhythm:

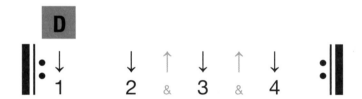

For the full syncopated effect, beat 2 here should be played lightly, and the offbeat between 2 and 3 should be emphasized. In fact, you can create an even more syncopated rhythm by also putting a phantom downstroke on beat 2…

Now simply omit the downstroke on beat 3, making sure that you still perform a 'phantom' downstroke instead (shown here in brackets).

…and even placing an extra upstroke between 1 and 2:

To play these rhythms fluently, it is vital to stick to the rule: downstrokes on the beat, upstrokes on the off-beat. This basic rule works for many styles, though for some the rate has to be double so there are four strokes per beat (down, up, down, up). For these exercises, tap your foot on the beat and imagine it is attached with string to your picking hand.

ON THE BEAT

Syncopation only works if the listener can identify where the beat is. If you are playing with a band where the bass and drums are playing mainly on the beat, you can play offbeats exclusively; some styles such as reggae and ska make heavy use of this idea. If you are playing on your own you will need to play on the beat at least once per bar, usually on beat 1 – otherwise all your upstrokes will sound like beats rather than offbeats.

SYNOCOPATED SONGS

These well-known songs use syncopated strumming patterns or riffs:

- Oasis: "Wonderwall"
- George Harrison: "My Sweet Lord"
- Van Morrison: "Brown Eyed Girl"
- Elvis Presley: "His Latest Flame"
- Kings Of Leon: "Use Somebody"

PRACTICE SEQUENCES

Try applying any of the three rhythms shown above to these chord sequences.

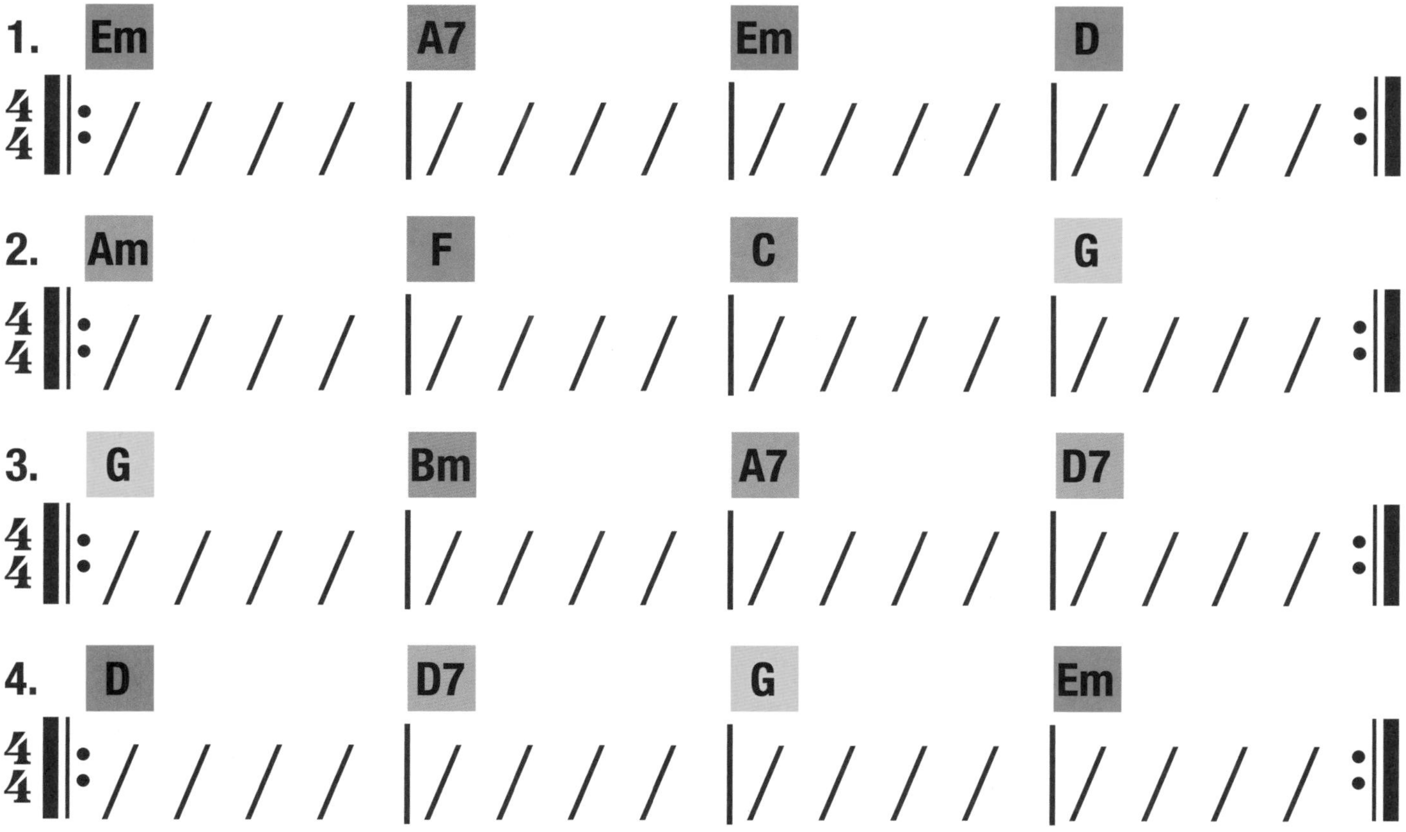

1. **Em** **A7** **Em** **D**

2. **Am** **F** **C** **G**

3. **G** **Bm** **A7** **D7**

4. **D** **D7** **G** **Em**

PLAY A SONG

Down By The Riverside

This simple spiritual song should be played reasonably fast, with a busy but relaxed right hand. Although written in $\frac{4}{4}$ here, above a certain tempo this begins to feel as though the main pulse is on beats 1 and 3. This is known as two feel or cut time. On the guitar, you might want to emphasize the bass strings a little more on these beats, while also accenting the full strums on beats 2 and 4. This should sound like a bass player and drummer working together.

CHORDS

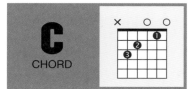

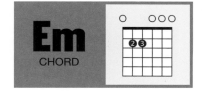

SUGGESTED STRUMMING PATTERN

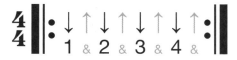

VERSE

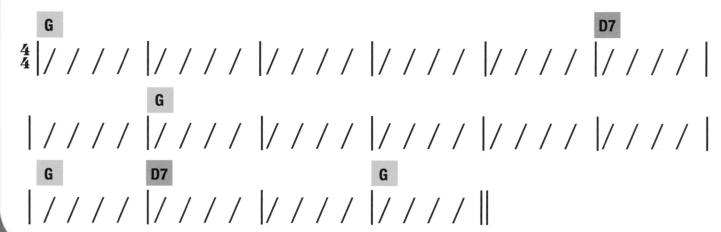

CHORUS

$\frac{4}{4}$

C		**G**		**D7**	
/ / / /	/ / / /	/ / / /	/ / / /	/ / / /	/ / / /

G		**C**		**G**	**Em**
/ / / /	/ / / /	/ / / /	/ / / /	/ / / /	/ / / /

D7	**G**		
/ / / /	/ / / /	/ / / /	/ / / /

VERSE 1

G

Gonna lay down my burden, Down by the riverside,

D7

Down by the riverside,

G

Down by the riverside.

Gonna lay down my burden, Down by the riverside,

D7   **G**

Down by the riverside.

CHORUS

C

I ain't gonna study war no more,

G

Ain't gonna study war no more,

D7   **G**

I ain't gonna study war no more.

C

I ain't gonna study war no more,

G   **Em**

Ain't gonna study war no more,

D7   **G**

I ain't gonna study war no more.

VERSE 2

I'm gonna lay down my sword and shield…

Repeat Chorus

VERSE 3

I'm gonna put on my long white robe…

Repeat Chorus

VERSE 4

I'm gonna try on my starry crown…

Repeat Chorus

VERSE 5

I'm gonna talk with the prince of peace…

Repeat Chorus

CHAPTER 6:

LEAD GUITAR AND ROCK 'N' ROLL

This is the type of playing that inspired many to take up the guitar in the first place. From Chuck Berry and Elvis Presley onwards, rock 'n' roll has been a dominant force for the last sixty years.

LEFT: Jimmy Page from Led Zeppelin

USING DISTORTION

Rock players use distortion (also called 'overdrive') some of the time; a few use it nearly all of the time, and some styles including heavy metal are built on it.

Originally, distortion was an accidental by-product of turning the amp up loud: there was just one volume control, and as you turned it up you got more volume, but also the sound began to 'break up'. Guitar players often had to turn their small amps up really loud to compete with other instruments (especially drums) but then found that they also began to like the distortion effect. Later, amp designers began to add a master volume control at the end of the signal path so you could use distortion at lower volumes too. Since then, preamp volume (which creates distortion) has usually been called 'gain'.

> **GUITAR TIP:** With your amp set to heavy distortion, your guitar's volume control will have little or no effect on your overall volume for most of its range, but it can be useful for reducing the amount of distortion.

TRY THESE SOUNDS...

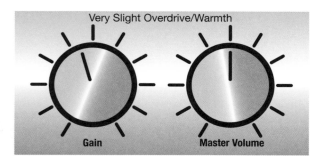

Very Slight Overdrive/Warmth
This essentially sounds like a clean sound but with a little more 'warmth', which is in fact very slight distortion.

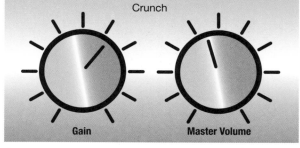

Crunch
'Crunch' means slight overdrive. Full chords are still clear, but with just a bit more edge and bite.

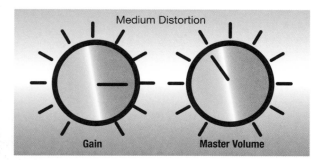

Medium Distortion
This amount of distortion begins to sound seriously rocky. With some guitars and amps, this could make full chords sound a bit congested, but it's great for power chords (p. 112) and riffs (p. 114).

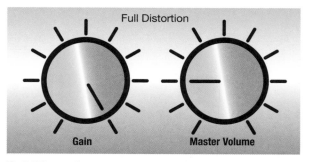

Full Distortion
This is the sound of heavy rock. You'll almost certainly want to avoid full major and minor chords, but power chords and riffs will sound great, and lead work will sing through nicely.

VALVE VS. TRANSISTOR

The classic rock distortion sound results from the design of the thermionic valve, or vacuum tube. This was the basic component in all amplifiers and many other electronic devices (including early computers!) until it began to be superseded by the transistor, which is smaller, cheaper and far more practical. In the 1970s and 80s, most amp manufacturers switched to transistor-based designs and were generally slow to react to the protests of guitarists who found the early transistor sound thin, brittle and unpleasant. Since then, designers have reintroduced valves and also found ways to improve the transistor sound.

Valve
The glass valve or tube (right) is at the heart of the rock guitar sound, while its more practical descendant the transistor (below) has not always replicated this well.

Transistor
An integrated circuit (silicon chip) may contain thousands or even millions of miniaturized transistors and is also an important part of modern amplifier design.

Clean and Overdrive Channels
The standard controls of a two-channel amp: the clean channel has a single volume control, while the overdrive channel has gain and volume. As you turn the gain up for more distortion, you will need to turn the volume down to stay at the same volume.

USING EFFECTS PEDALS

Effects pedals are small tone-shaping circuits that you can use (usually between the guitar and amp) to change the sound. They can usually be powered either via battery or an external power supply. A huge number of different sounds is available – here are some of the most popular choices.

DELAY/ECHO

This creates an echo effect using a variable delay. As the delayed sound always comes in after a fixed amount of time, this can be great for creating rhythmic effects. Delay is also used to create the 'slap back' (very short delay) sound associated with early rock 'n' roll. Most delay pedals have a number of different controls including delay time, mix (the balance between the original and delayed signals) and feedback (allowing the delayed signal to be fed back into the input, so you get multiple delays).

MODULATION EFFECTS

Delay Pedal
Some players have built their styles on the use of rhythmic delays, notably U2's The Edge.

Chorus
Perfect for 'taming' guitar sounds that would otherwise stand out too much.

Modulation effects such as Chorus, Flanging and Phasing all sound similar but are different. In all cases, a slow waveform is generated and modulated with the guitar signal to create some kind of 'sweeping' or 'whooshing' effect. This can be anything from very subtle to very obvious, is often used in pop rhythm guitar and was particularly popular in the 1980s.

Overdrive
Technically the same thing as distortion, but 'overdrive' is often used to describe chunky distortion sounds perfect for rock rhythm parts.

Distortion
If you don't have distortion on your amp, you can add a great distortion sound with a pedal like this classic BOSS model.

Reverb
This effect adds a sense of space around your guitar sound.

DISTORTION

Though distortion can be created by your amp, there are many reasons for using distortion pedals too. Firstly, there are different kinds of distortion sounds, so using pedals lets you switch between them while using the same amp. Secondly, though some amps have several channels and a footswitch for switching between clean and distortion sounds, many do not. Thirdly, some effects (notably chorus) sound much better if placed after any distortion – with some amps, using a distortion pedal may be the only way to achieve this.

REVERB

This simulates either the effect of playing in a reverberant space such as a concert hall or cathedral, or the sound of some of the vintage devices that were themselves designed to emulate this effect but have a character all their own (such as 'spring' and 'plate' reverbs).

Cry Baby
The quintessential (and perfectly named) wah pedal.

WAH-WAH

This pedal can be used to make the guitar sound as though it is talking or crying, by rocking the foot back and forth as you play (the top plate is connected to a kind of tone control). This is particularly associated with psychedelic rock and some styles of funk, and was popularized by Jimi Hendrix and Eric Clapton in the late 1960s.

INTRODUCING NOTATION & TABLATURE

The simple strumming patterns we have encountered up to this point are not capable of notating anything very much more complicated. Lead guitar (playing single-note melodies), like other melodic instruments, requires precise notation of notes and rhythms.

There are two systems for notating guitar music: standard notation, which uses the symbols seen in classical music scores or sheet music, and tablature (often known as tab). Parts for use by professional players only ever use standard notation, but many books and guitar publications use both simultaneously.

STANDARD NOTATION

All instruments in Western music share the system of standard musical notation. This means that it is possible to play music written for the violin or flute (for example) on the guitar. Standard notation uses a system of five lines called a stave, and the spaces between them, to show the pitches of notes, together with a system of notating rhythm.

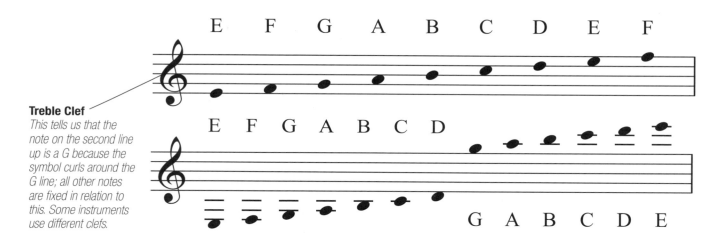

Treble Clef
This tells us that the note on the second line up is a G because the symbol curls around the G line; all other notes are fixed in relation to this. Some instruments use different clefs.

Notes above and below this range are shown using temporary lines called *leger lines* – as many as necessary.

NOTE DURATIONS

Symbol	American	British	Duration in 4/4
o	Whole note	Semibreve	4 beat
♩	Half note	Minim	2 beat
♩	Quarter note	Crotchet	1 beat
♪	Eighth note	Quaver	½ beat

In 4/4, note durations are shown as follows:
Consecutive quavers (half beats) are usually beamed together in groups of two or four:

There is also a system of symbols telling us not to play for a given amount of time. These are called rests:

RESTS

Symbol	American	British	Duration in $\frac{4}{4}$
▬	Whole note	Semibreve	4 beats
▬	Half note	Minim	2 beats
𝄽	Quarter note	Crotchet	1 beat
𝄾	Eighth note	Quaver	½ beat

TABLATURE

On many instruments, there is only one way to play any given note. On the guitar however, it can be hard to know where to play the notes you are reading, as there may be up to four feasible places to find it. The system known as tablature tells us where to find notes on the guitar, using six horizontal lines (one for each string; the lowest represents the low E string). Numbers represent fret numbers.

In the example above, the first note is found on the low E string, 1st fret. The second note is found on the A string, 3rd fret. The third note is the open D string (O = open).

Though tablature is useful for telling us where to find *notes*, it tells us nothing about the rhythm. In guitar music, however, both systems are often used simultaneously.

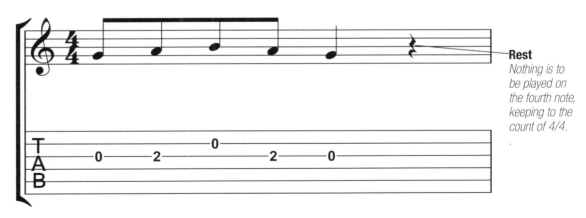

Rest
Nothing is to be played on the fourth note, keeping to the count of 4/4.

In the example above, the notation stave tells us that the notes G, A, B, A, G are played in the rhythm '1 & 2 & 3' with a rest on beat 4; the TAB stave tells us where to find these notes.

MELODIC PLAYING AND LEAD GUITAR

Whereas playing chords usually involves fairly expansive right-hand strumming, melodic playing tends to use small right-hand movements, with the base of the palm resting somewhere on or around the bridge, and only moving from the wrist.

Picking
The right hand often rests lightly on the bridge when picking, but should still be free to make larger movements if necessary.

Like strumming, picking ultimately involves both up- and downstrokes, but let's get started with a simple exercise using downstrokes only: the C major scale in first position. In the first exercise we're playing the notes C, D, E, F, G, A, B, C on the strings A, D, G & B.

First position means that the first finger should be used for all notes at the first fret, the second finger for all notes at the second fret, and so on. Make sure that all notes in the scale sound clearly; in particular, make sure that the fingers of the left hand do not accidentally press on other strings.

This scale can be used to play some simple versions of well-known melodies. Can you identify them?

INTRODUCING 'THE' ROCK 'N' ROLL PATTERN

This highly useful rhythm guitar idea is associated with early rock 'n' roll, and Chuck Berry in particular; it is sometimes known as the Chuck Berry Shuffle, and is usually transposed through the twelve-bar blues sequence, which forms the basis of most rock 'n' roll songs.

This idea is easiest to play in the key of A, where it essentially consists of 'rocking' back and forth between two notes on the same string, while also playing the open string below. So instead of playing an A or A7, we can play this pattern:

To transpose this to work where we see a D chord, simply move this idea to the next pair of strings:

And for the E chord, it shifts down to the lowest string pair:

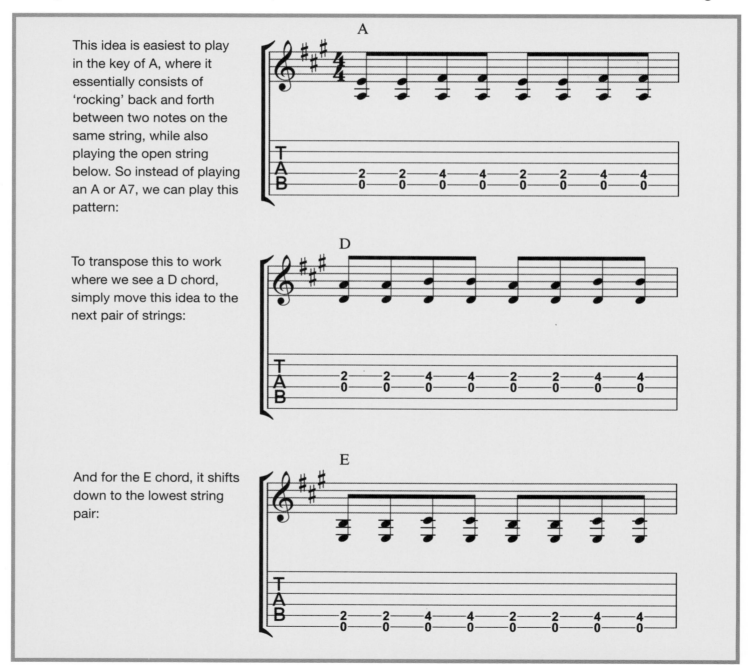

THE ROOTS OF ROCK 'N' ROLL

For many, the defining moment of rock 'n' roll occurred in 1954 when Elvis Presley, Scotty Moore and Bill Black recorded Arthur Crudup's "That's All Right", fusing blues and white country music together. Bill Black reportedly remarked, 'Damn. Get that on the radio and they'll run us out of town.' At this point the American musical audience was segregated along racial lines. To others, rock 'n' roll was simply an appropriation of a black musical style (rhythm 'n' blues) by white musicians; black artists then merely applied the label to their existing style. In hindsight, there is some truth to both thoughts.

SHARPS, FLATS & KEY SIGNATURES

If a musical piece is in a key other than C major or A minor, it will generally use notes known as sharps and flats (the black notes on the piano). A sharp note is shown using a sharp sign ♯ and a flat note using a flat sign ♭. Often, it is easier to place a number of sharp or flat symbols at the beginning of each line, telling us which notes are to be sharpened or flattened throughout. This also tells us instantly what the key is, so it is known as the *key signature*. The examples here are all in A major, so there are three sharp signs in the key signature telling us that instead of F, C and G we have to play F♯, C♯ and G♯.

95

GUITAR HEROES

JIMI HENDRIX
1942–1971

RECOMMENDED LISTENING:
Are you Experienced? (album)
Axis: Bold as Love (album)
Electric Ladyland (album)

Jimi Hendrix was born in Seattle, Washington. He was a completely self-taught guitarist and learned by imitating his heroes. These included blues greats such as Muddy Waters and Albert King, soul musicians such as Curtis Mayfield, and saxophonist Rahsaan Roland Kirk.

Hendrix revolutionized rock music in the four years before his death, pushing back boundaries with his effects-laden, feedback-soaked rock 'n' roll and wild stage shows, and it all began the day his father bought him his first guitar for $5 from a junk shop.

After a brief spell in the Army, Hendrix moved to Nashville to play in its various blues clubs with his companion Billy Cox. He soon found work as a stand-in guitarist for bands such as the Isley Brothers and that of Little Richard. In 1966 Jimi moved to London to form The Jimi Hendrix Experience with bassist Noel Redding and drummer Mitch Mitchell. The trio's first single, "Hey Joe," was an instant hit and with the release of his debut album, *Are You Experienced?* Hendrix was catapulted to fame. In 1967 Hendrix returned to the United States, where a performance at the Monterey Pop Festival won him international recognition.

Hendrix pioneered the use of distortion, feedback and effects units such as the wah-wah pedal. He blended funk, rock and blues effortlessly, creating some of the most passionate and soulful rock guitar ever recorded. In 1970 Hendrix died of a sleeping pill overdose, but his legacy continues to this day. His influence is obvious in the music of many well-known musicians, including Prince, Lenny Kravitz, Hawksley Workman, Slash and Stevie Ray Vaughan.

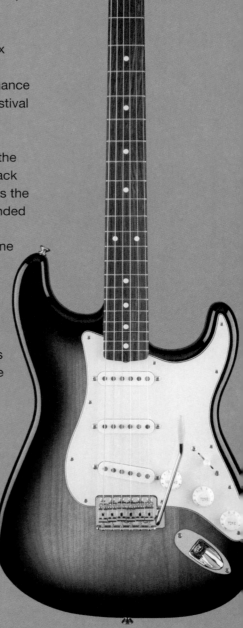

Fender Stratocaster
Jimi Hendrix is a major factor in the iconic status of this guitar.

FAVOURED GUITARS:

FENDER STRATOCASTER

Lefty
Hendrix played a right-handed Strat re-strung for left-handed playing.

PLAY A SONG

Blame It On The Blues

This song by Ma Rainey comes from the very dawn of The Blues. You could either play it using open seventh chords, or using the Rock 'n' Roll shuffle pattern shown on p. 95: when A7 is shown here, play the A pattern, and so on.

CHORDS

CHORD SEQUENCE

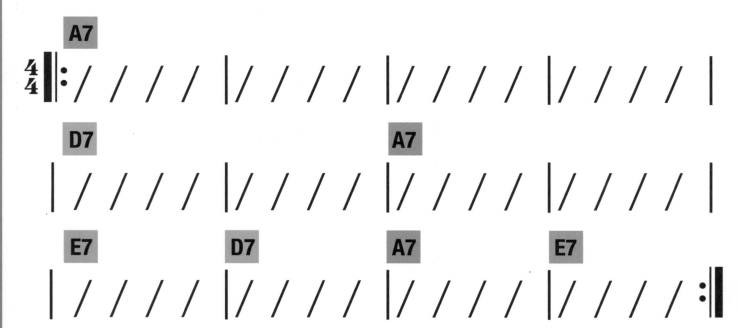

VERSE 1

A7

I'm so sad and worried, got no time to spread the news,

D7   **A7**

I'm so sad and worried, got no time to spread the news.

    E7   **D7**   **A7**

Won't blame it on my troubles, can't blame it on the blues.

VERSE 2

A7

I can't blame my daddy, he treats me nice and kind,

D7   **A7**

I can't blame my daddy, he treats me nice and kind.

    E7   **D7**   **A7**   **E7**

Shall I blame it on my nephew, blame it on that trouble of mine?

VERSE 3

    A7

This house is like a graveyard when I'm left here by myself,

    D7   **A7**

This house is like a graveyard when I'm left here by myself,

    E7   **D7**   **A7**   **E7**

Shall I blame it on my lover? Blame it on somebody else.

VERSE 4

A7

  Can't blame it on my mother, can't blame my dad,

  Can't blame my brother for the trouble I've had.

D7

  Can't blame my lover, that held my hand,

A7

  Can't blame my husband, can't blame my man.

E7   **D7**   **A7**   **E7**

  Can't blame nobody, guess I'll have to blame it on the blues.

CHAPTER 7:

FINGERSTYLE GUITAR

The guitar is an incredibly versatile and varied instrument. Here we take a look at the subtler side of the acoustic guitar.

LEFT: John Martyn

INTRODUCING FINGERSTYLE GUITAR

The core skills in rock and pop guitar playing involve using the pick as we have seen up to this point. However, there is another strand of guitar playing that involves using the thumb and fingers of the right hand individually. Fingerstyle technique is mainly associated with the acoustic guitar.

In guitar music, the following abbreviations, which come from traditional Spanish words, are sometimes used to denote right-hand fingering:

p (*pulgar*) = thumb

i (*indice*) = index finger

m (*medio*) = middle finger

a (*anular*) = ring finger

GUITAR TIP: For the best sound, the fingernails of the right hand should be used rather than the flesh of the fingertips.

For most simple fingerstyle picking ideas, the thumb plays the bass strings while the next three fingers cover the treble (highest three) strings. For the fingerstyle patterns on this page, the index finger should play all notes on the G string, the middle finger on the B string and the ring finger on the high E string. The thumb plays all notes on the bass strings (low E, A and D) and the fourth finger is generally not used.

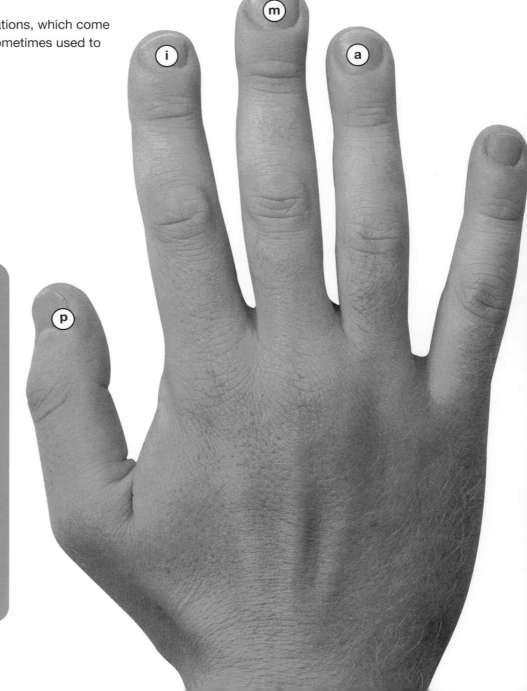

ONE AT A TIME

The simplest and generally most effective picking pattern involves *arpeggiating* the notes of a chord, which means to play them one at a time. Usually this involves beginning with a bass note and progressing up and then down through the strings, though many types of pattern are possible. The pattern below uses a C major chord that is held throughout. Make sure that all the notes are picked with the right-hand fingers indicated and, most importantly, that all notes are allowed to ring on from the time they are played until the end of the bar.

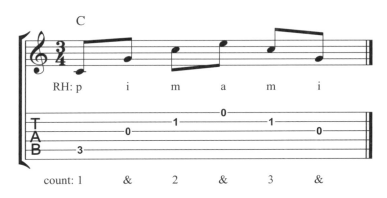

GUITAR TIP: Once this simple arpeggiated pattern feels comfortable, try varying it by playing the same notes in a different order. It's usually best to start with the bass note, but after this you can try many other variations – for example, change 'i m a m i' to 'a m i m a'. You could also try playing the thumb and ring finger (top string) together on the first beat. This is called a *pinch.*

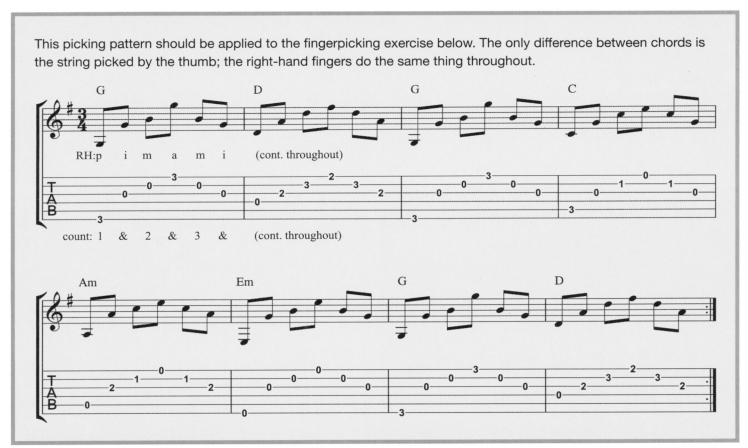

FOLK AND CLASSICAL GUITARS

This kind of pattern is also often found in classical guitar (see p. 106). Apart from using a different instrument, classical guitar differs from folk guitar in that this is not the only kind of right-hand technique used, and that the right hand often plays melodies as well as accompaniment, or combines the two.

MORE FINGERSTYLE PATTERNS

The time signature of $\frac{3}{4}$ lends itself to arpeggiated fingerstyle patterns that simply proceed up and then back down for each chord, such as those discussed on p. 102–103. As most popular music is in $\frac{4}{4}$ however, more complex patterns are often needed.

GUITAR TIP: When playing with another guitarist, try achieving a more complex texture by doing different things with the same chord sequence. For example, one of you could play arpeggios, as shown here, while the other strums. If you have the means to record your playing, why not try playing both parts yourself? Recording is an excellent form of practice; don't be surprised if you don't like the sound you hear. Instead, try to work out how you can improve it.

The right hand is in position for all the picking patterns shown here. The thumb covers the bass strings while the first three fingers cover one treble string each.

The following examples show some possibilities for arpeggiating a C major chord in $\frac{4}{4}$.
The exercises below use two of these patterns with popular chord sequences.

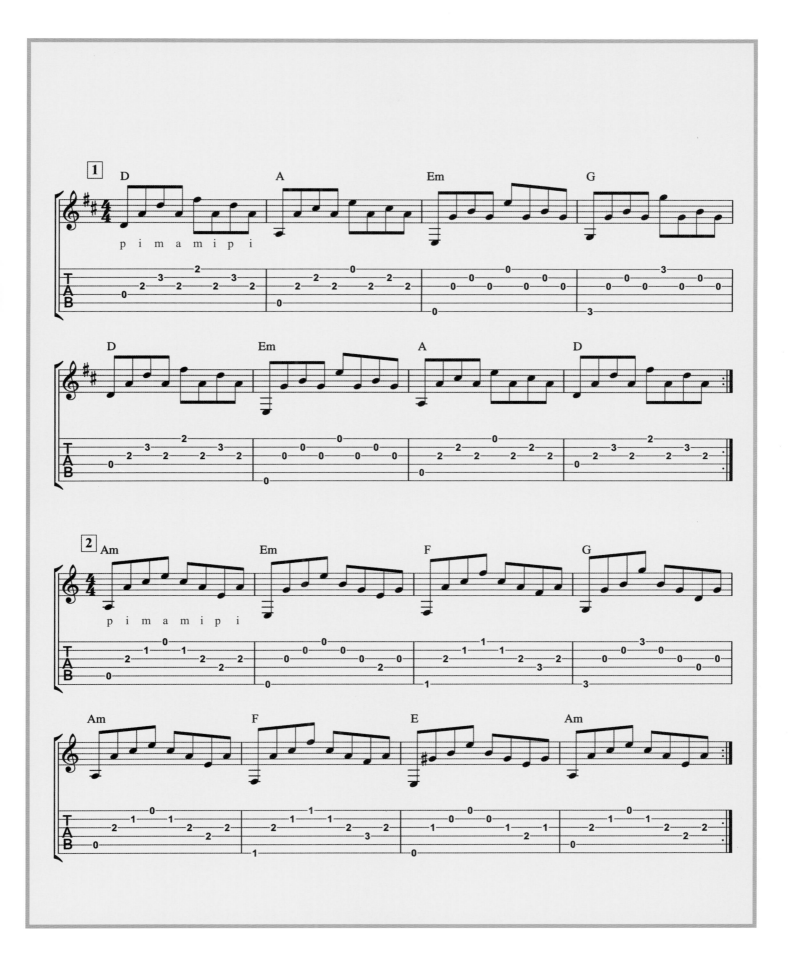

105

A TASTE OF CLASSICAL GUITAR

'Classical guitar' may refer to a type of instrument: essentially, an acoustic guitar with nylon strings (the bass strings look like steel strings, but they are actually made of many strands of nylon with a soft metal winding). Though this instrument, also known as the Spanish guitar, can be used to play melodies and chords in many styles of music, it is most associated with a style all its own: classical guitar music, often with a strong Spanish influence.

At a beginners' level, classical guitar technique is similar to fingerstyle guitar technique: the right-hand thumb is often used to cover the basic strings and the first three fingers often play arpeggiated chords on the treble strings. In more advanced playing, the fingers may be used to play melodically too. Classical players never use a pick.

NOTATION

Classical guitar music is almost always written without tablature or chord symbols; some fingering information is usually included, however.

Sitting Position
Whereas rock and pop players are fairly relaxed about posture, classical players and teachers are much more specific. The guitar is placed on the left leg, which is raised by means of a foot stool, resulting in the angle shown here.

For compatibility with the rest of this book, the piece below is written in standard notation and tab. For this piece, the thumb should play the lower strings and the fingers i, m and a should play the G, B and E strings as discussed on p. 102. Left-hand fingerings are shown using numbers 1, 2, 3 and 4 (and O: open string).

Sometimes fingers will have to stay in place in order to ring on as shown. This piece moves in semiquavers (sixteenth notes) throughout: count these '1 e & a 2 e & a 3 e & a 4 e & a'. You may need to start at a slow tempo to play these smoothly and on this piece one bar at a time at first.

PIECE – OP. 50 NO 1 BY MAURO GIULANI (1781–1829)

HYBRID PICKING

While pure fingerpicking tends to be the province of acoustic players (most electric players play with a pick), there is a compromise, that is often used on both electric and acoustic guitar, particularly in Latin jazz and country music: hybrid picking.

Hybrid picking involves holding the pick between the thumb and first finger as usual, but also picking the strings with the remaining fingers. Many hybrid pickers use the fourth finger, allowing them to play any pattern that a 'pure' fingerstyle player would play using the thumb and first three fingers.

In both Latin and country music, however, the fingers are often used all together. This can be used to create punchy patterns consisting of a bass line and rhythmic chords, sounding a bit more like a piano than a picked or strummed guitar.

Both of the examples below use the C major chord, but involve moving the third finger to the low E string, 3rd fret. Bass notes (the single notes here) are played with the pick, while the higher chords are played with the 2nd, 3rd and 4th fingers together.

Basic Hybrid Picking Position
The pick covers the bass strings while the remaining fingers take care of the upper strings.

FINGERPICKS

Steel strings can be pretty unforgiving to play, causing the fingernails to wear down and break. Some players, particularly in country music, solve this by using individual picks known as fingerpicks. These can be made of metal or plastic, and essentially function as nail extensions. Using these can feel unnatural at first, as the fingers have to adopt slightly different angles and the fingerpicks can easily get stuck on the strings if you don't get it right. Some players use the thumb pick only: this gives the advantages of hybrid picking without having to use the little finger.

Playing with Fingerpicks
When using fingerpicks the thumb is used in more of a sideways approach, as shown here (right).

CHAPTER 8:

ROCK GUITAR

Rock begins where rock 'n' roll leaves off, and often draws on a wider range of influences.

LEFT: Jason Newsted and James Hetfield of Metallica

INTRODUCING POWER CHORDS

The overdriven guitar sound is rich in harmonics: higher frequencies mathematically related to the notes played. Full major and minor chords can sound heavily congested and dissonant as all these harmonics tend to 'fight'. For this reason, rhythm guitar parts with heavy distortion tend to use simpler chords known as power chords.

THE ROOT AND THE FIFTH

Power chords contain just two notes: the root – which gives a chord its name – and the fifth (major and minor chords contain a third between these two notes, which determines whether the chord is major or minor). So power chords are also known as '5' chords: A5, E5 etc.

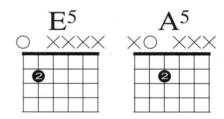

Try the exercises below with heavy distortion. To achieve this, turn your amp's gain control up to a high setting. You'll probably want to bring the master volume control down to compensate for the increased volume.

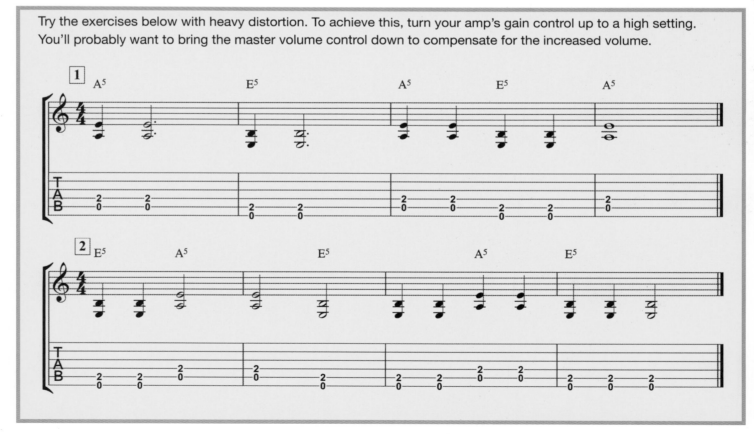

The simplest power chords may be played with one fretted finger (the fifth) and one open string.
Note: a dot placed after any note adds half as much again to its duration. So the dotted minims (half notes that are two beats long) above are worth three beats.

MOVEABLE POWER CHORDS

Two fingers are needed to play moveable power chords. Usually, the root is on either the low E string or the A string. In the boxes right 'fr3' means that the first fret shown is the third fret, so the first finger should be at the third fret and the third finger at the fifth fret. The following exercises combine open and moveable power chords.

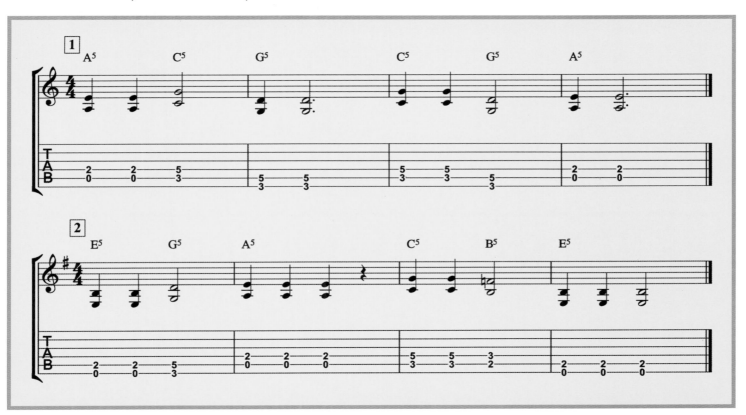

POWER CHORD SONGS

Black Sabbath:	"Paranoid"
Dire Straits:	"Money For Nothing"
The Kinks:	"You Really Got Me"
The Rolling Stones:	"(I Can't Get No) Satisfaction"
Deep Purple:	"Smoke On The Water"
Green Day:	"Basket Case"
The Ramones:	"Blitzkrieg Bop"
Blur:	"Song 2"
Nirvana:	"In Bloom"

RIFFS

A riff is a simple instrumental figure that underpins a rock song. A great riff can be as important and memorable as the song's vocal melody or lyrics. Many great riffs stay around the bottom of the guitar's range, and use single notes or power chords. A catchy riff can make a song instantly recognizable.

In the following exercises, all notes should be played using downstrokes except for pairs of quavers that should be played down and then up (down on the beat, up on the offbeat).

If you find this difficult at first, you could try tapping your foot on the beat. Then, imagine that your foot is connected to your picking hand like a puppet on a string, making it impossible for them to move in opposite directions.

CLASSIC RIFFS

The Beatles:	**"Day Tripper"**
Free:	**"All Right Now"**
David Bowie:	**"Rebel Rebel"**
T. Rex:	**"20th Century Boy"**
AC/DC:	**"Back In Black"**
Aerosmith:	**"Walk This Way"**
U2:	**"Desire"**
Metallica:	**"Enter Sandman"**

EXERCISES

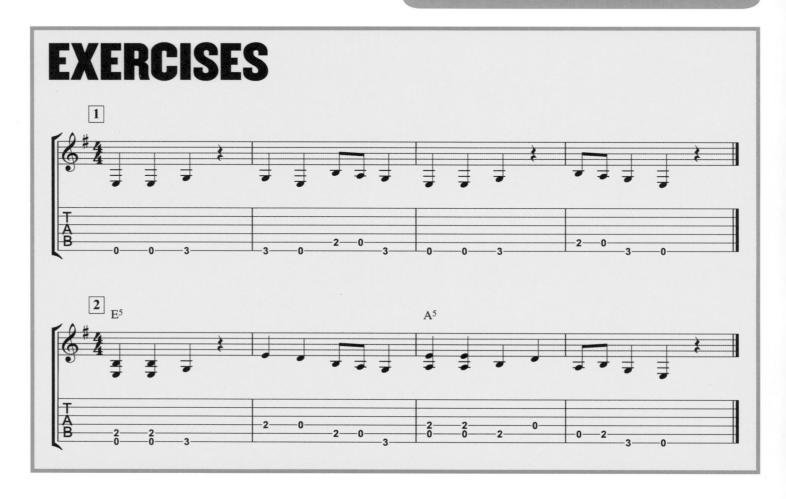

BLUES BENDS

Many rock riffs in E and A use a device called a blues bend. This involves physically bending a string (see left) to raise its pitch very slightly for a bluesy flavour. In low guitar riffs, blues bends are often added to the note G (low E string, 3rd fret).

The riff exercises below use blues bends. Blues bends are usually notated as quarter-tone bends (half a semitone, or half the interval from one fret to the next), but in a bluesy context this is approximate.

EXERCISES

PALM MUTING

Palm muting is a right-hand technique used to stop the strings from ringing and sounding fully to make a more percussive, muffled sound while still (usually) containing an identifiable pitch. Palm muting is used in many styles including funk, disco, reggae and rock.

The whole palm is not really used. Rather, the flesh at the side of the right hand (fourth finger side) rests just inside the bridge. Here, we can control the amount of sound produced from the strings. A very small difference in position can have a great effect on the sound. This allows for a great degree of creative control over both the level and tone of the sound produced.

Palm muting is usually shown using the letters 'P.M.'. In rock, palm muting is often used to produce 'chugging' rhythm patterns using power chords.

Palm Muting
The side of the hand is used to mute the strings, in this case near the bridge.

EXERCISES

Releasing palm muting can be used to produce powerful accents, as the sound will automatically be louder and fuller when the muting is released. The exercise below applies this to E-shape barre chords in the key of E. (It is difficult to mute a whole six-string chord, so only the lowest two notes are played when muting is applied here – a two-note power chord.)

Where Did You Sleep Last Night?

This traditional song (also known as "In The Pines") has been recorded by many artists including legendary bluesman Lead Belly and, more recently, Nirvana.

CHORDS

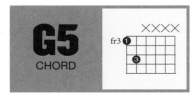

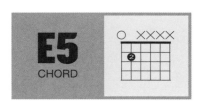

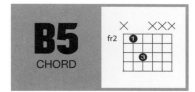

SUGGESTED STRUMMING PATTERN

VERSE

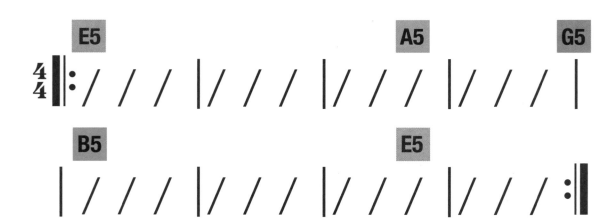

VERSE 1

E5   A5 G5   B5   E5

My girl, my girl, don't lie to me – tell me where did you sleep last night?

      E5   A5   G5

In the pines, in the pines, where the sun don't ever shine,

      B5   E5

I would shiver the whole night through.

VERSE 2

E5   A5   G5 B5   E5

My girl, my girl, where will you go? I'm going where the cold wind blows.

      E5   A5   G5

In the pines, in the pines, where the sun don't ever shine,

      B5   E5

I would shiver the whole night through.

VERSE 3

  E5   A5 G5   B5   E5

Her husband, was a hard working man, just about a mile from here.

E5   A5   G5

His head was found in a driving wheel,

      B5   E5

But his body never was found.

Repeat Verses 1 & 2

GUITAR HEROES

BILLIE JOE ARMSTRONG

1972–

RECOMMENDED LISTENING:
Dookie (album)
American Idiot (album)
21st Century Breakdown (album)

Billie Joe Armstrong is best known as the guitarist and singer in the punk rock band Green Day.

Green Day have been one of the most successful rock acts in the world since the mid 1990s, and were key players in the resurgence of the punk ideal at around that time: simple songs in a forceful style, with direct (often political) lyrics mirrored by an aggressive sound of high gain guitar and pounding drums.

Green Day's early style was characterized by simple riffs using power chords, often relying on fast repetitive downstrokes for energy – as heard on the frantic early hit "Basket Case". This kind of riff is actually deceptively hard to maintain through the course of a song at such a fast tempo. Even in their early work, Green Day occasionally stepped away from this barrage of sound to develop another side of their music, for example the acoustic guitar and string quartet of "Good Riddance (Time Of Your Life)". Later work has broadened the power trio's sound in a more pop direction to include keyboards and a more 'produced', layered sound. Their most successful album, 2004's *American Idiot*, formed the basis for a successful Broadway musical of the same name.

More recently Armstrong has explored broader musical directions, notably 2013's *Foreverly*, on which he and Norah Jones faithfully reworked the Everly Brothers' country music classic *Songs Our Daddy Taught Us* – in American music, possibly the polar opposite of the sound and ethos of Green Day.

Les Paul Junior
Armstrong's favourite guitar, the Gibson Les Paul Junior, has just a bridge pickup – perfect for cutting through a punk track.

FAVOURED GUITARS:

FENDER STRATOCASTER
TELECASTER
JAZZMASTER
GIBSON LES PAUL JUNIOR

PLAYING IN A BAND

Even if you are enjoying learning the guitar on your own, the ultimate aim for most aspiring players is to perform with others. This can be a hugely enjoyable experience, but can also come with its own frustrations. Here are a few things worth thinking about.

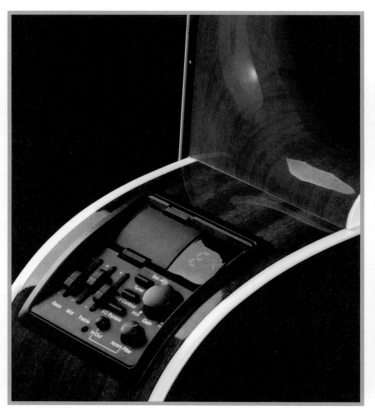

Tools and Tuners
Left: this electro-acoustic guitar features useful sound-shaping tools and an integrated tuner.

Magnetic Pickup
Below: this magnetic pickup attaches to a standard acoustic guitar with metal strings to enable amplification.

VOLUME

Practice amps are rarely loud enough on their own to cut it against several other instruments, especially if these include drums – and the acoustic guitar certainly isn't! There are several possible solutions depending on the type of guitar you have and the amount of volume you need.

For electric guitar, the easiest solution here is usually to get a bigger amp. Amps suitable for playing with a full rock band are usually rated at least 50W (watts), though this is only a very rough rule of thumb. Tube (valve) amps in particular can sometimes be very loud even if they are rated much lower than this.

If you are particularly attached to the sound of an existing amp that isn't quite loud enough, you can feed its sound through the band's PA (public address) system in one of two ways: either by placing a microphone in front of it, or via a direct connection. Be aware that the sound of the electric guitar as we know it (particularly with distortion) is partly a product of the way guitar speakers are made: to put it simply, they are inherently lo-fi devices. So a direct input (also known as DI) to a PA system may result in a rather different sound from that coming from your speaker. On the other hand, your amp may have a special circuit designed to emulate the sound of a guitar speaker: look for terms like 'speaker emulation' or 'emulated output' on the rear panel.

Acoustic guitars are simpler in this respect. The best way to amplify an acoustic guitar (unless you have a dedicated acoustic amplifier) is using a pickup and feeding the signal to the PA system. Many acoustics have an integrated pickup system: these are known as electro-acoustic guitars. Pickup solutions are also available for fitting to standard acoustic guitars.

PROTECT YOUR HEARING

As soon as drums are involved in a musical situation, volumes can get really loud. Exposure to these high volumes can permanently damage your hearing. It is therefore a sensible idea to wear earplugs. If you are worried that you won't be able to hear what's going on properly, don't be: earplugs can actually have the opposite effect. At the sort of volume that can damage hearing, what we are hearing actually begins to distort in our ears, making it hard to hear what is going on and causing severe fatigue. So earplugs often make it easier to hear the whole band, by removing this in-ear distortion, and making the whole experience less tiring.

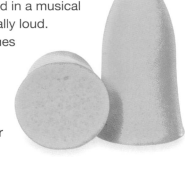

Earplugs
Even cheap disposable earplugs like these can be a life-saver in loud environments.

KEEP IT SIMPLE

It is much better to play something simple, and do it well, than to play complex parts badly. One of the most important things for a band is to sound as though you are all playing in time with each other, and this is much easier to achieve with simple ideas. Most rock and pop songs have simple chord sequences; most of the time the role of the guitarist is to supply this harmonic backdrop without drawing too much attention from the main focus, which is usually the vocal line.

LISTEN TO OTHERS

Try to listen, constantly, to what the other players are doing. In particular, listen to the drums and try to play perfectly in time with them. The timing of most pop and rock music is dictated by the snare drum. This is the really loud drum that goes 'crack', usually on beats 2 and 4 in every bar. This is known as the backbeat. Some of the most effective guitar parts work around the backbeat by avoiding playing on beats 2 and 4, so that the snare can punch through here.

RECORD YOURSELVES

One of the best ways to learn as a musician is to record yourself and listen critically to your own playing. This applies to groups as much as individuals. For more advice on recording, see p. 124.

Practice Makes Perfect
In a band rehearsal, try to make sure all players can see each other.

RECORDING

There are many reasons why you might want to record your guitar playing. For one thing, it's a great way to get a clear view of your progress as a player. Listening to recordings of yourself can be highly revealing (and sometimes depressing, even for really accomplished players). Beyond this, you might want to record yourself or your band playing songs.

HARDWARE

To make a simple guitar recording, the simplest thing is to use a dedicated solid state recorder with an integrated microphone. These generally record to SD card or internal memory, and recordings can easily be transferred to your computer for editing.

Portable Power
Even a basic laptop can run some very powerful recording software.

Handy Hardware
A basic mixer may be a useful addition to a computer recording set-up. A mixer processes sound so you can equalize it – highs, mids and lows – as well as add effects (echo, reverb, delay).

The Missing Link
This basic audio interface acts as a bridge between your guitar and computer.

For more sophisticated recording capability, you will need all or most of the following:

- A computer (Mac/PC) or tablet
- An audio interface
- One or more microphones
- Recording software

COMPUTER OR TABLET
Almost any computer or tablet (or even smartphone) will be capable of running some sort of recording software; more powerful machines will be able to run powerful professional software while tablets generally lack sufficient power.

While it is possible to use your computer or tablet's integrated audio connections, for better results you will need some form of audio interface.

AUDIO INTERFACE
This is simply a box connected to your computer or tablet to provide audio connections: from one input and one output to hundreds of channels, depending on your requirements and budget. It is important to check whether your chosen interface is compatible with your hardware and operating system, and that it has the right inputs and outputs for you: in particular, you will probably want at least one microphone input; many interfaces also have a high impedance ('hi-Z') input for direct connection of your guitar.

MICROPHONES
You can record electric guitar by pointing a relatively inexpensive dynamic microphone such as a Shure SM57 straight at the amp, usually right up close. This technique is used by many professional recording engineers. For recording acoustic guitar, you may wish to spend a little more on a condenser microphone.

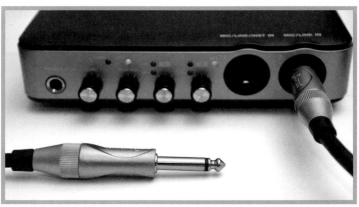

SOFTWARE
There are many free or inexpensive apps for simple recording. For more advanced recording, editing and mixing (including multi-track recording and integrated virtual instruments and effects) you will need a piece of software called a Digital Audio Workstation (usually abbreviated to DAW). As well as the full, professional versions of these programs, many are available in 'lite' versions, most of which are still surprisingly powerful.

- Avid Pro Tools
- Apple Logic Pro
- Steinberg Cubase

If you are using a direct connection to your audio interface (bypassing the amp and microphone), your electric guitar won't sound like an electric guitar unless you use a plug-in (piece of software running within the DAW) designed to emulate the effect of amplification. There are many such amp emulation plug-ins available, and most of them include emulations of dozens of amps and effects pedals. This is a great way to experience the possibilities of different effects without a hefty investment in pedals.

CHAPTER 9:

CHORD REFERENCE

This chapter is a library of chords arranged logically to provide beginners with a convenient reference point collecting together the chords you need to play more of the kinds of songs found in this book.

C CHORDS

C

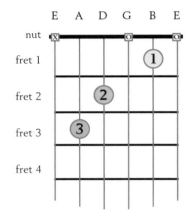

C (alternative)

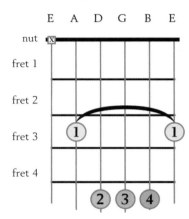

C7

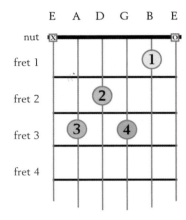

Cmaj7

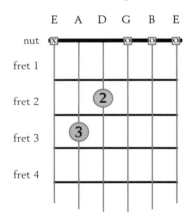

Cm

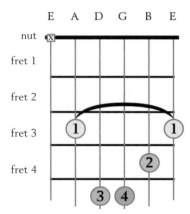

Cm (alternative)

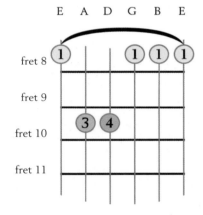

Cm7

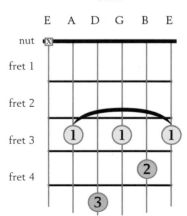

C6

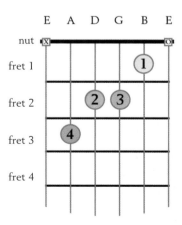

C9

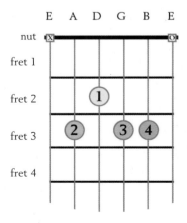

C# CHORDS

C#

E A D G B E

nut

fret 1

fret 2

fret 3

fret 4

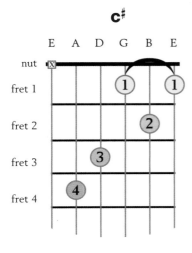

C# (alternative)

E A D G B E

fret 3

fret 4

fret 5

fret 6

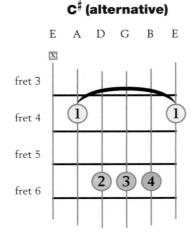

C#7

E A D G B E

fret 2

fret 3

fret 4

fret 5

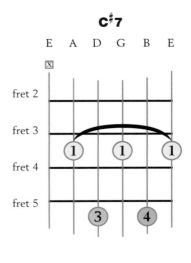

C#maj7

E A D G B E

fret 2

fret 3

fret 4

fret 5

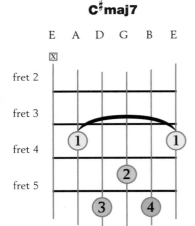

C#m

E A D G B E

fret 3

fret 4

fret 5

fret 6

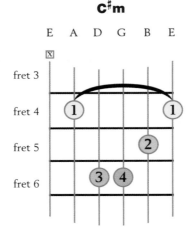

C#m (alternative)

E A D G B E

fret 8

fret 9

fret 10

fret 11

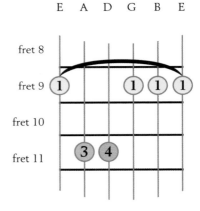

C#m7

E A D G B E

fret 4

fret 5

fret 6

fret 7

SHARP AND FLATS

C#=D♭

E♭=D#

F#=G♭

A♭=G#

B♭=A#

A chord name that includes a sharp (#) or flat (♭) symbol is built on one of the black piano keys. All of these have two possible names; you should bear this in mind when searching for a chord. Depending on the context, the black key may be named after the white key immediately above, or the one immediately below. For example, the note between C and D may be called C# or D♭. In chord symbols, this means that a C# chord is physically the same as a D♭ chord. This applies to all chord types - for example, C#m7 could also be called D♭m7.

D CHORDS

D

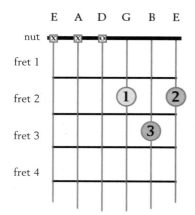

D (alternative)

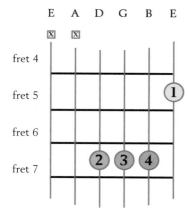

D7

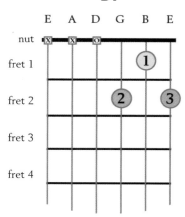

Dmaj7

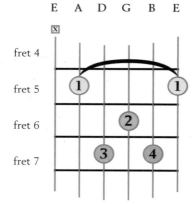

Dm

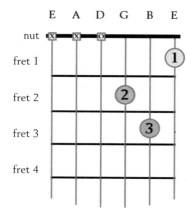

Dm (alternative)

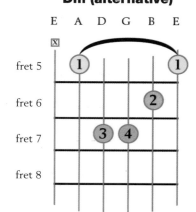

Dm7

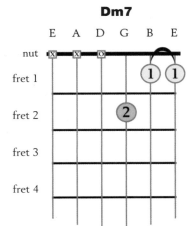

D6

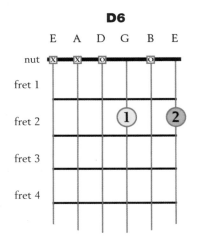

D9

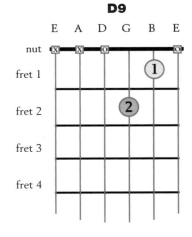

E♭ CHORDS

| ① | = FIRST FINGER | ② | = SECOND FINGER | ③ | = THIRD FINGER | ④ | = FOURTH FINGER | ⓞ | = OPEN STRING | ☒ | = DO NOT PLAY THIS STRING |

E♭

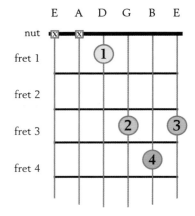

E♭ (alternative)

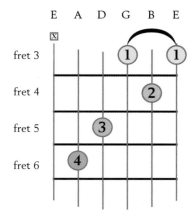

E♭7

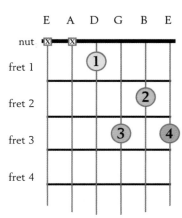

E♭maj7

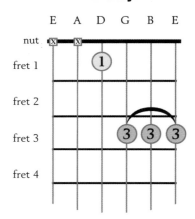

E♭m

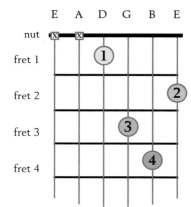

E♭m (alternative)

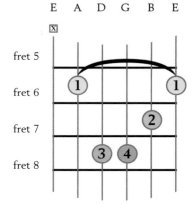

E♭m7

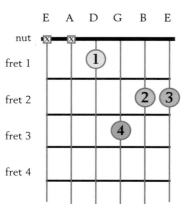

E CHORDS

E
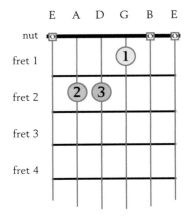

E (alternative)
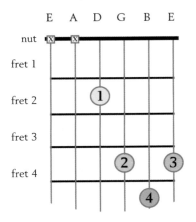

E7
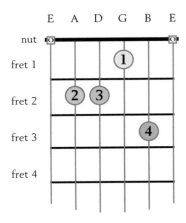

Emaj7
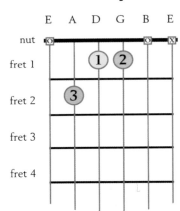

Em
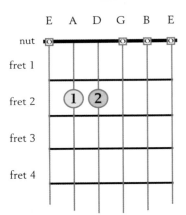

Em (alternative)
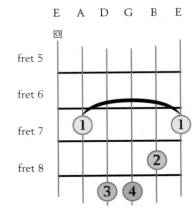

Em7
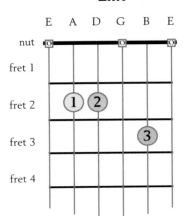

E6
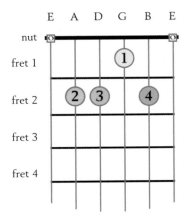

E9
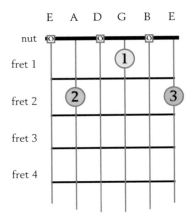

F CHORDS

F
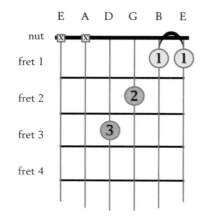

F (alternative)
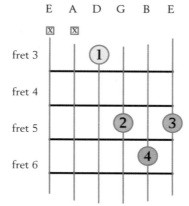

F (alternative)
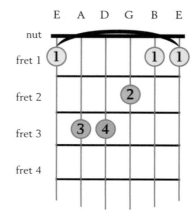

F7
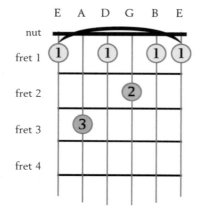

Fmaj7
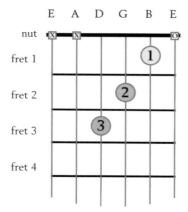

Fm
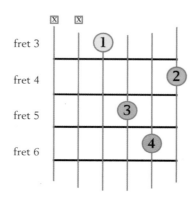

Fm (alternative)
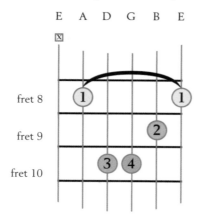

Fm (alternative)
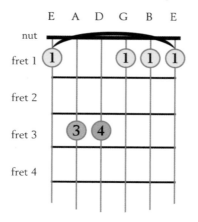

Fm7
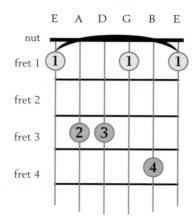

F♯ CHORDS

F♯

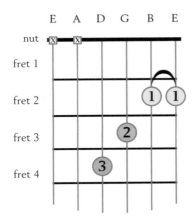

F♯ (alternative)

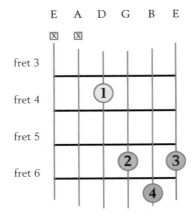

F♯7

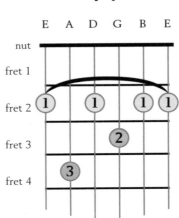

F♯maj7

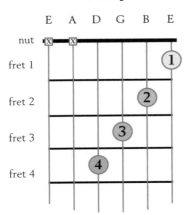

F♯m

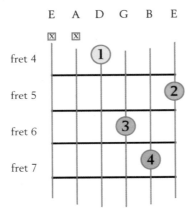

F♯m (alternative)

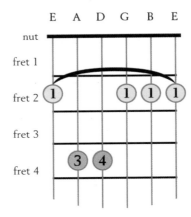

F♯m7

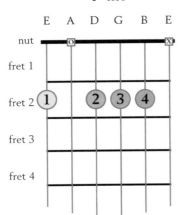

G CHORDS

G

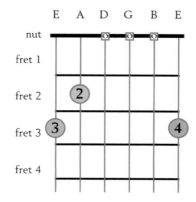

G (alternative)

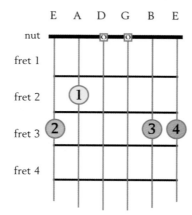

G (alternative)

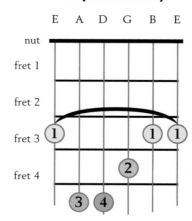

G7

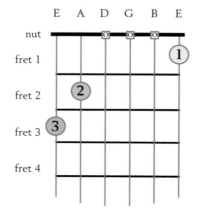

Gmaj7

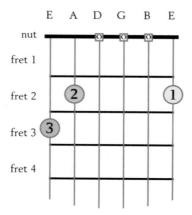

Gm

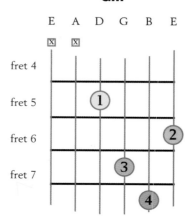

Gm (alternative)

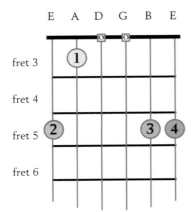

Gm (alternative)

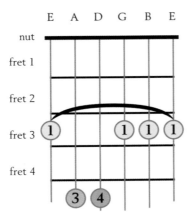

Gm7

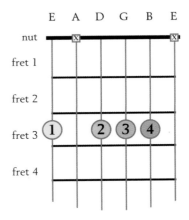

G6

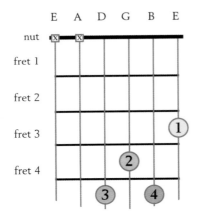

G9

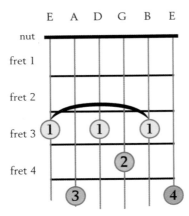

A♭ CHORDS

A♭

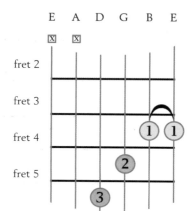

A♭ (alternative)

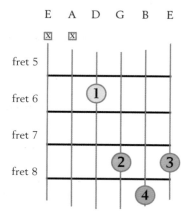

A♭7

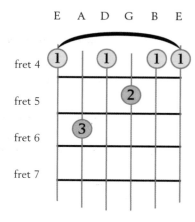

A♭maj7

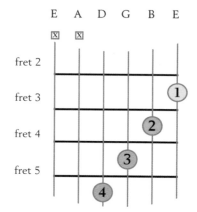

A♭m

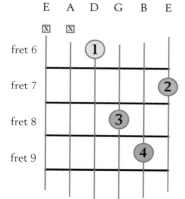

A♭m (alternative)

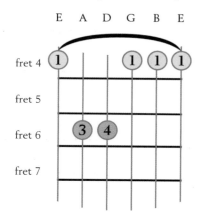

A♭m7

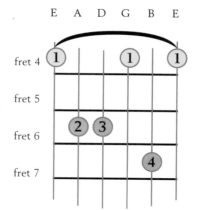

A CHORDS

A

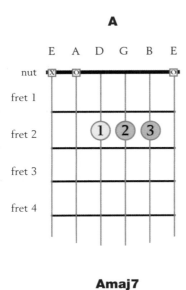

A (alternative)

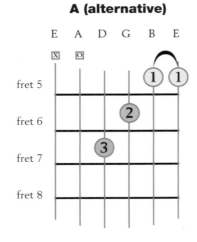

A7

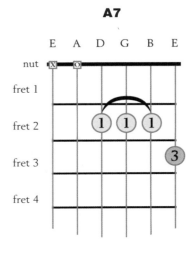

Amaj7

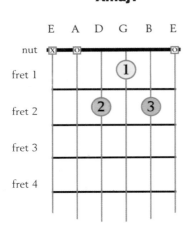

Am

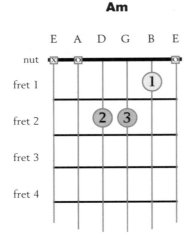

Am (alternative)

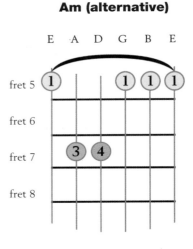

Am7

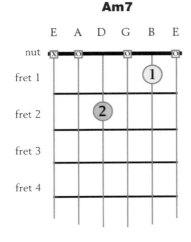

A6

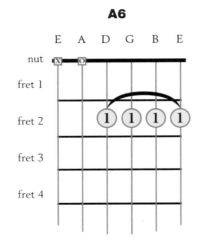

A9

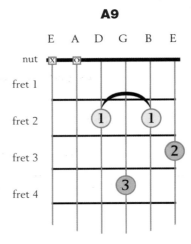

B♭ CHORDS

B♭

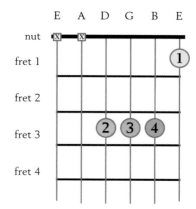

B♭ (alternative)

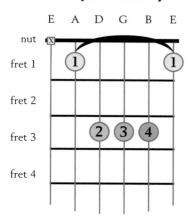

B♭7

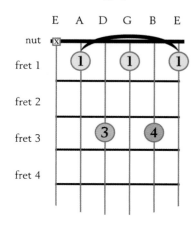

B♭maj7

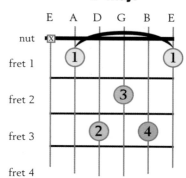

B♭m

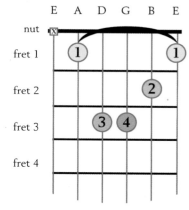

B♭m (alternative)

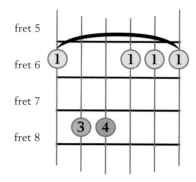

B♭m7

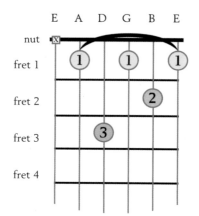

B CHORDS

B

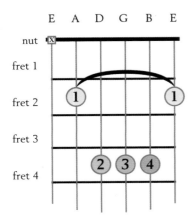

B (alternative)

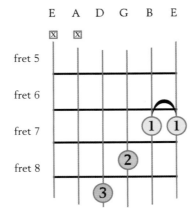

B7

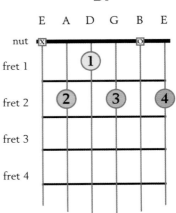

Bmaj7

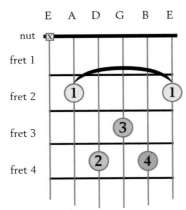

Bm

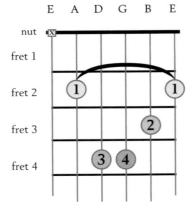

Bm (alternative)

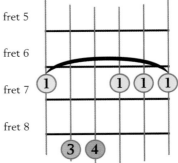

Bm7

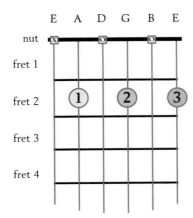

GLOSSARY

Accented Note
A note played with more emphasis than others.

Arpeggio
The notes in a chord played one at a time rather than all together.

Amplifier
A device that increases the strength of the electrical signal coming from the guitars pickups. Stronger signal, louder sound.

Augmented
A perfect interval that has been increased by a semitone. For example, a perfect fifth is an interval of 7 semitones, therefore an augmented fifth is an interval of 8 semitones.

Bar
A subdivision of time in music.

Barre
Using your finger to hold down more than one string at one fret in a single chord, in order to build chords using that fret as the 'nut'.

Bass
Sounds of a lower frequency.

Bend
Raising the pitch of a note by pushing the string sideways across the fretboard.

Blues bend
Bending a string to raise its pitch very slightly for a bluesy sound. In low guitar riffs, blues bends are often added to the note G (low E string, 3rd fret).

Blue note (flattened fifth)
The minor third, diminished fifth and flat seventh of a key. The tension between the 'blue notes' and the regular notes of the major scale is a key factor in the blues sound.

Body
The main part of a guitar (excluding the neck).

Bridge
The bridge is located on the body of the guitar and transfers sound from the strings to the body of the guitar.

Capo
A device which clamps onto the fretboard acting as the nut.

Chord
Three or more pitches played simultaneously, usually a root, third and fifth.

C (Common time)
The symbol "C" used as a time signature; another name for $\frac{4}{4}$ time.

Diminished Chord
A chord consisting of a minor third and a diminished fifth. For example a D diminished chord contains D, F and A flat.

Distortion
A guitar effect in which gain (an increase in power of a signal) is used to create a dirty and fuzzy sound. There are many forms of distortion, used in various styles of music.

Echo
A single reflection of sound that is heard after the direct sound. Any extra distance the sound has to travel adds to the time delay. An echo is a distinct reflection of sound and is not to be confused with reverberation.

Effects Pedals
Devices that use sound processors to achieve a desired sound.

Flat
Flat generally just means lower. The flat of the note you are on would be one semitone lower. To tune flat, you 'tune' 'down'.

Fingerpicking
A pattern-based way of playing through chord progressions using the fingers.

Fifth (note of a chord)
In a scale, the distance between a certain note and another note four notes above it. The certain note is counted as I, the note four notes above that is V.

Fretboard
The fretted surface of the neck where you press down the strings.

Fret
Technically, the frets are the small metal bars across the neck of your guitar or bass. When you press your fingertip down between two 'frets' you will fret the string and make the appropriate corresponding note. (You do not press your fingertip 'on' the frets, but between them).

Gain
The amount of increase in power a signal is exposed to. Determines the amount of distortion and sustain.

Harmony
Two or more pleasing notes sounding simultaneously.

In Tune
A note is in-tune when it matches the pitch of another note in the manner it is supposed to. When tuning a guitar, strings are 'in tune' with each other when you can sound the same note on different strings and they sound the same. When playing a chord, a note is in tune if it sounds at the right interval from the other notes around it.

Key
The tonal center of a piece of music.

Major
This is a type of scale or chord that sounds bright, happy and upbeat. It has no flats in it.

Melody
A succession of musical notes played one after another (usually the most recognizable tune of a song).

Minor
This is a type of scale or chord that sounds dark, maybe sad and gloomy. Minor scales or chords do use flats.

Muting
A technique used to muffle the ringing of notes, done with the edge of the palm.

Neck
The part of a guitar that houses the fret board.

Nut
The nut is placed at the end of the fingerboard and controls the strings spacing, distance from the edge of the fingerboard and their height above the first fret.

Octave
An interval of 12 semitones.

Offbeat
An unaccented beat in the bar.

Onbeat
The first and third beats in a bar of four-four time.

Open
A string played with no left hand finger fretting any note.

Open Chord
A chord that contains open strings.

P.M. (Palm Muting)
A technique used to muffle the ringing of notes, done with the edge of the palm.

Pentatonic Scale
A scale with only 5 tones. There are two standard pentatonic scales: major and minor.

Pickup
The electronic device used to pick up the sound of electric guitar strings. There are many types and configurations.

Position
The four frets that your hand is over at any given time. 'Position' also refers to the pattern of notes to be played at any four frets for your chosen scale.

Pick
A small, triangular-shaped piece of plastic used for striking the guitar strings with the hand.

Pitch
The frequency of a note (how high or low it sounds).

Resonator
The circular speaker-like device that fits into the body of some guitars, used to increase volume.

Reverb
A constant wave of overlapping echoes producing an ambient effect.

Rhythm
A sequence of events played with the right hand on a guitar, which gives a piece of music a distinct beat.

Riff
A repeated sequence of notes, most common in rock and pop.

Root note
The note from which a scale or chord is based. The first note of a scale or chord.

Scale
A group of notes that work well together.

Seventh
In a scale, the distance between a certain note and another note six notes above it. The certain note is counted as I, the note six notes above that is vii.

Sharp
Sharp generally means higher. The sharp of the note you are on would be one semitone higher. To tune sharp, you tune 'up'.

Sound Hole
The hole in the centre of the soundboard that allows the sound to travel out of the guitar.

Strumming
A technique where the right hand plays the notes of a chord simultaneously, either with down or up strokes.

Syncopation
Using accents on some of the weaker beats to create a more diverse rhythm.

Swing
A rhythm in music in which the downbeat is felt slightly longer than the upbeat (sometimes called a shuffle).

Tablature
A pictorial system of notation for guitar music, showing six strings and fret positions.

Tempo
The overall speed of a piece of music.

Third (note of a chord)
In a scale, the distance between a certain note and another note two notes above it. The certain note is counted as I, the note two notes above that is iii.

Tone
The combination of pitch, volume, sustain and sound character produced by a particular guitar or guitar equipment.

Tuning
Adjusting the tuning pegs until a particular string vibrates at the correct frequency, and sounds the proper note(s).

Tuning peg
A knob used to tighten or loosen a string. The effect is to raise or lower the pitch to bring the string into proper tune.

Vibrato
A wavering sound produced by shivering a fretted note up and down rapidly.

INDEX

A
A chords 138–9
  A (major) 22, 32–3, 34–5, 52–3, 138–9
  A5 112, 118–19
  A7 54–5, 62, 64–5, 98–9, 139
  A♭ 138
  A minor (Am) 40–1, 44–5, 52–3, 54–5, 76–7, 139
acoustic guitars 7, 78
  and amplifiers 122
  changing strings 43
  fingerstyle technique 102–9
  magnetic pickup 122
  parts of 16
  strings 42, 43
  tuners 13
  vs electric guitar 12
amplifiers
  cables 15
  choosing 14
controls 21
distortion 86–7
effects pedals 88–9
Marshall Stack 7
plugging in 21
practice amps 14
valves vs. transistors 87
volume 14, 122
wattage 14, 122
apps
  tuner 13
  metronome 25
  recording 125
Armstrong, Billie Joe 120–1, 121
arpeggiating 103, 104–5
Asus2 chord 40
audio interface 125
Aura Lea 64–5

B
B chords 140–1
  B (major) 53, 140–1
  B5 118–9
  B7 60–1, 64–5, 141
  B♭ 140
B minor (Bm) 74–5, 141
backbeat 123
bands, playing in 122–5
barre chords 72–7
bars 23
Beatles, The 126–7
beats
  backbeat 123
  metronomes 25
  musical notation 90–1
  offbeats 51, 80–1
  syncopation 80–1
  time signature 23
Beautiful Dreamer 54–5
Blame in on the Blues 98–9
blues 60–1, 66–7
blues bends 115
Bugg, Jake 26–7, 27

C
C chords 128–9
  C (major) 36–7, 38–9, 41, 44–5, 53, 76–7, 82–3, 128–9
  C5 113
  C7 128–9
C♯ 129
  C minor (Cm) 128
cables 15, 21
capos 68–9
cases 15
CF Martin & Co 7
changing chords 31, 33, 41
chord boxes 22
chords 128–41
  5 chords 112–13
  barre 72–7
  blues 66–67
  building 53
  changing between 31, 33, 41
  chord boxes 22
  definition of 19
  power 112–13
  reference library 128–41
  seventh 54–55, 60–63, 64–65, 66–67, 98–99
  tonic 30
  see also individual chords
Chuck Berry Shuffle 94–5
classical guitar
  changing strings 43
  posture 106

strings 42, 43
technique 106–7
classical strings 42, 43
computers, for recording
    124–5

D
D chords 130–1
    D (major) 30–1, 33, 34–5,
        38–9, 41, 44–5, 52–3,
        76–7, 130–1
    D7 54–5, 63, 64–5, 82–3,
        98–9, 130–1
    D minor (Dm) 130–1
delay pedal 46, 88
distortion 86–7
    pedals 89
Down by the Riverside 82–3
drums 123

E
E chords 132–3
    E (major) 32–3, 34–5, 41,
        52–3, 132–3
    E5 12, 118–19
    E7 62, 64–5, 76–7, 98–9,
        132–3
    E♭ 132
    E minor 23–5, 38–9, 41,
        44–5, 52–3, 64–5, 82–3,
        132–3
earplugs 123
echo effect 88
effects pedals *6*, 88–9
    software 125
electric guitars
    amplifiers 14
    changing strings 43
    parts of *17*
    strings 42, 43
    tuners 13
    vs acoustic guitar 12

F
F chords 134–5
    F (major) 53, 73, 76–7,
        134–5
    F7 134–5
    F♯ 135
    F minor (Fm) 73, 134–5
Fender
    Stratocaster *96*
    Telecaster *26*
fingerpicking *see* fingerstyle
guitar
fingerpicks 109
fingers
    abbreviations 102
    fingerpicks 109
    fingerstyle guitar 102, 104
    ...d picking 108–9

numbering of 22
position of 19, 72
sore 7, 12
fingerstyle guitar 102–9
    hybrid picking 108–9
five chords 112–13
flats 95, 129
flattened fifth 67
fretboards *16, 17,* 19
    capos 68–9
    fretboard dots 75

G
G chords 136–7
    G (major) 36–7, 38–9, 41,
        44–5, 52–3, 54–5, 64–5,
        82–3, 136
    G5 113, 118–19
    G7 136–7
    G minor (Gm) 136–7
ghost strokes 51
Gibson
    J-45 *78*
    Les Paul *6*
    Les Paul Junior *120*
gig bags 15
Giulani, Mauro 107
Green Day 120–1

H
Haim, Danielle *70–1*
hands *see* fingers
harmonics 75
Harrison, George *7*
hearing, protection of 123
Hendrix, Jimi 96–7, *97*
Hetfield, James *110–11*
Holly, Buddy *28*
House of the Rising Sun
    76–7
hybrid picking 108–9

J
jack cables 15, 21
jack plugs 15, 21

K
key signatures 95
King, B.B. *7*

L
lead guitar 90–3
left hand, position of 19
Les Paul *6*
Les Paul Junior *120*
Little Martin (guitar) *46*
looper pedal 46

M
magnetic pickup 122
major and minor chords 23, 53

Marley, Bob *48–9*
Marshall Stack *7*
Martyn, John *100*
Mayer, John 56–7, *57*
melodic playing 90–3
Metallica *110–11*
metronomes 25
microphones 125
minor pentatonic scale 67
mixers 125
modulation effects 88
muting 116–17

N
National Resonator guitar 67
Newsted, Jason *110–11*
notation 90–5, 106–7
notes
    duration of 90–1
    position on clef 90
    rests 91
    symbols 90
    tablature 91
nylon strings 42, 43, 106

O
offbeats 51, 80–1
Oh! Susanna 38–9
OMJM John Mayer *56*
overdrive 86–7
    pedals 89

P
PA system 122
Page, Jimmy *84*
palm muting 116–17
Passenger (Mike Rosenberg)
    78–9, *79*
pedals, effects *6,* 46, 88–9
phantom strokes 51
picking 92–3, 102–9
    classical guitar 106–7
    hybrid picking 108–9
picks 13, 19, 51, 92, 108–9
plectrums *see* picks
posture 18–19, 106
power chords 112–13
practice amplifiers 14
practice sessions 7

R
reading music 24, 90–5
recording 124–5
reggae 51
repeats 24
resonator guitars 67
rests 91
reverb 89
rhythm guitar, power chords
    112–13
riffs 114–15

right hand, position of 19
rock guitar 112–21
rock 'n' roll pattern 94–5
Rosenberg, Mike 78–9, *79*

S
seventh chords 54–5, 60–3,
    64–5, 66–7, 98–9, 128–40
sharps 95, 129
Sheeran, Ed 46–7, *47*
software, for recording 125
Spanish guitar 106–7
stands 15
steel strings 42, 109
steel-strung guitars *see*
acoustic guitars
straps 13, 18
strings
    changing 42–3
    classical 42, 43
    names of open strings 20
    nylon 42–3, 106
    steel 42, 109
    types of 42
strumming 19
    alternating strokes 50–2
    exercises 24–5
    phantom/ghost strokes 51
    syncopation 80–1
    upstrokes 50–2
Swing Low Sweet Chariot
    34–5
syncopation 80–1

T
tablature 90–5
tempo, metronomes 25
thumbs, position of 19
time signatures 23, 24
tonic chords 30
transistors, amplifiers 87
treble clef 90
tuners 13, 20
tuning 20
Turner, Alex *8*
twelve bar blues 66–7

U
upstrokes 50–2
    syncopation 80–1

V
valves, amplifiers 87

W
wah-wah pedal 89
Water is Wide, The 44–5
Waters, Muddy *58–9*
*Where Did You Sleep Last
    Night?* 118–19
White, Jack *6*